"I could not put this book down. Dr. Fajgenbaum is an inspiration, and *Chasing My Cure* is a page-turning chronicle of living, nearly dying, and discovering what it really means to be invincible in hope."

—ANGELA DUCKWORTH, *New York Times* bestselling author of *Grit*

"This book is so gripping that I read it in one sitting—and so moving that I can't stop thinking about it months later. It's an extraordinary memoir, filled with wisdom, by a doctor who came face-to-face with his own mortality. It belongs in rare company with Atul Gawande's writings and *When Breath Becomes Air*." —ADAM GRANT, *New York Times* bestselling author of *Give and Take* and *Originals* and co-author of *Option B*

"*Chasing My Cure* is a medical thriller that grapples with supreme stakes—real love, bedrock faith, and how we spend our time on earth. Fast-paced and achingly transparent, David Fajgenbaum's deeply thoughtful memoir will have you rethinking your life's priorities."

—LYNN VINCENT, *New York Times* bestselling author of *Indianapolis* and co-author of *Heaven is for Real*

"This is a riveting story of a remarkable journey of one persevering through illness to medical discoveries and recovery. It's a tribute to Dr. Fajgenbaum's rare qualities of spirit and intellect, the support of his family and friends, the power of modern science, and the role that patients can play to find new treatments. *Chasing My Cure* is mesmerizing."

—J. LARRY JAMESON MD, PhD, dean of the Perelman School of Medicine, University of Pennsylvania

"This is a fascinating true-life story of a young doctor who, stricken with a rare, life-threatening disease, takes matters into his own hands and, with total focus, finds a cure. . . . An informative and inspiring read."   —ANDREW WEIL, MD

"I was riveted from the very first to the very last page of this extraordinary story of life, assumed death, resilience, and hope. I am convinced that through his incredible journey, David Fajgenbaum has acquired 'superpowers' that will no doubt shape the lives of others, now and well into the future."

—NICOLE BOICE, founder of Global Genes

"*Chasing My Cure* is an extremely powerful story about turning fear into faith and hope into action. David Fajgenbaum's ferocious will to survive and his leadership in the face of his rare disease provide a model pathway for others to follow when searching for cures of their own."

—STEPHEN GROFT, PharmD, former director of the Office of Rare Diseases Research, National Institutes of Health

"A remarkable and gripping story of how a potentially fatal and rare illness inspired the patient to commit himself as a physician/scientist to search for its cause and cure. Dr. Fajgenbaum's description of his journey is a tale of courage, dedication, and brilliance that will enthrall and fascinate its readers."

—ARTHUR H. RUBENSTEIN, professor of medicine, the Perelman School of Medicine, University of Pennsylvania

"Inquiring physicians have discovered much from studying patients with rare diseases, but rarely has the physician been the patient. Dr. Fajgenbaum tells the remarkable story of his own mysterious, nearly fatal multisystem disease and his brilliant deduction that a long-known drug may be the cure. This book—part detective story, part love story, part scientific quest—shows how one indefatigable physician can bring hope to patients who suffer from a rare disease that is barely on the radar screen of medical science."

—MICHAEL S. BROWN, MD, recipient of
the Nobel Prize in Medicine, 1985

"David Fajgenbaum, a self-proclaimed 'rare disease quarterback,' shares with us his extraordinary story of assembling a team and a framework to conduct unprecedented collaborative research. In his deeply personal memoir, he makes plain the urgency of hope, and explores how the human spirit might transcend suffering to inspire communities to take collective action against seemingly insurmountable odds."

—JOHN J. DEGIOIA, president, Georgetown University

"Dr. Fajgenbaum has taken a tragic personal situation and turned it into a story that provides a model for all those who want to improve treatment of rare disease. Indeed, the lessons are not only good for people concerned about rare disease, but also for anyone dealing with illness or considering doing something to change the biomedical science enterprise."

—ROBERT M. CALIFF, MD, former commissioner,
U.S. Food and Drug Administration

CHASING MY CURE

CHASING MY CURE

A DOCTOR'S RACE TO TURN
HOPE INTO ACTION

A MEMOIR

DAVID FAJGENBAUM

BALLANTINE BOOKS

NEW YORK

Published in the United States by Ballantine Books, an imprint of
Random House, a division of Penguin Random House LLC, New York.

BALLANTINE and the HOUSE colophon are registered trademarks
of Penguin Random House LLC.

LIBRARY OF CONGRESS CATALOGING-IN-PUBLICATION DATA
Names: Fajgenbaum, David C., author.
Title: Chasing my cure : a doctor's race to turn hope into action : a memoir
/ David Fajgenbaum, M.D.
Description: First edition. | New York : Ballantine Books, [2019]
Identifiers: LCCN 2019011796 (print) | LCCN 2019012931 (ebook)
| ISBN 9781524799625 (Ebook) | ISBN 9781524799618 (hardback)
Subjects: LCSH: Fajgenbaum, David C.,—Health. | Lymph nodes—
Cancer—Patients—United States—Biography. | Physicians—Diseases—
United States. | Physicians—United States—Biography.
| BISAC: BIOGRAPHY & AUTOBIOGRAPHY /
Personal Memoirs. | PHILOSOPHY / Mind & Body.
| SOCIAL SCIENCE / Death & Dying.
Classification: LCC RC280.L9 (ebook) | LCC RC280.L9 F35 2019 (print)
| DDC 616.99/4460092 [B] —dc23
LC record available at https://lccn.loc.gov/2019011796

Printed in the United States of America on acid-free paper

randomhousebooks.com

4 6 8 9 7 5 3

Book design by Jo Anne Metsch

I would like to dedicate this book to my mom, my dad, my sisters, and Caitlin and Amelia. You taught me how to live, supported me when I was dying, and inspired me to chase cures for my disease and others. I love you.

CHASING MY CURE

AFTER YOU'VE MASTERED the basics of technique—hand placement, head tilt, and timing—and after you've accepted the inevitable feeling of shattering ribs beneath the heels of your hands, the hardest thing about performing CPR is knowing when to stop.

What if one more pump could do it?

Or one more after that?

When—no matter how hard you push, how hard you hope and pray—that pulse just will not return, then what comes next is entirely up to you. The life has already been lost. But hope hasn't been, not necessarily. You could keep *that* alive at least. You could keep doing compressions until your arms and shoulders are too worn out to continue, until you can't push hard enough to make a difference, much less break another rib.

So—how long do you try to bring someone back?

Eventually you will remove your hands from the body, eventually you'll have to—but *eventually* isn't a number. It isn't guidance. You won't see it in a CPR diagram. And it doesn't even really answer "when" so much as "why." When you *eventually* stop, you stop because there's no more hope.

That's what makes the decision so difficult. Your effort allows you to hope that life is possible, and your hope inspires you to push even harder. The three of those things—hope, life, and effort—chase one another, keep one another moving around a track.

I have performed CPR twice in my life. Both times, the patients were nearly dead when I began my relentless chest compressions and prayers. And both ended up dying. I didn't want to stop. I wish I was still going right now. And I continued to hope that I'd see a pulse appear on the heart monitor even after I had stopped my chest compressions. But hoping and wishing are often not enough. Hope can be a force; but it isn't a superpower. Neither is any part of medicine, much as we'd like it to be.

It can feel like one, though.

When I set out to be a doctor, I had already borne witness to incurable disease and inconsolable sadness—my mother had died of brain cancer when I was in college—but I was still optimistic about the power of science and medicine to find answers and cures. Because to be honest, long after I could reasonably blame it on youth and naïveté, I basically believed in the Santa Claus theory of civilization: that for every problem in the world, there are surely people working diligently—in workshops near and far, with powers both practical and magical—to solve it. Or perhaps they've already solved it.

That faith has perverse effects, especially in medicine. Believing that nearly all medical questions are already answered means that all you need to do is find a doctor who knows the answers. And as long as Santa-doctors are working diligently on those diseases for which there are not yet answers, there is no incentive for us to try to push forward progress for these diseases when they affect us or our loved ones.

I know better now. I've had a lot of time over the past few years to think about doctors, and they've had a lot of time to think about me. One thing I've learned is that every one of us who puts on a white coat has a fraught relationship with the concept of *authority*. Of course, we all train and grind for years and years to *have* it. We all *want* it. And we all seek to be the trusted voice in the room when someone else is full of urgent questions. And the public expects near omniscience from physicians. But at the same time, all of that education, all those books, all those clinical rotations, all of it instills in us a kind of realism about what is and what is not ultimately possible. Not one of us knows all there is to know. Not even nearly. We may perform masterfully from time to time—and a select few may really *be* masterful at particular specialties—but by and large we accept our limits. It's not easy. Because beyond those limits are mirages of omnipotence that torture us: a life we could have saved, a cure we could have found. A drug. A diagnosis. A firm answer.

The truth is that no one knows everything, but that's not really the problem. The problem is that, for some things, no one knows *anything, nothing* is being done to change that, and sometimes medicine can be frankly wrong.

I still believe in the power of science and medicine. And I still believe in the importance of hard work and kindness. And I am still hopeful. And I still pray. But my adventures as both a doctor and a patient have taught me volumes about the often unfair disconnect between the best that science can offer and our fragile longevity, between thoughts and prayers and health and well-being.

This is a story about how I found out that Santa's proxies in medicine didn't exist, they weren't working on my gift, and they wouldn't be delivering me a cure. It's also a story about how I came to understand that hope cannot be a passive concept. It's a choice and a force; hoping for something takes more than casting out a wish to the universe and waiting for it to occur. Hope should inspire action. And when it does inspire action in medicine and science, that hope can become a reality, beyond your wildest dreams.

In essence, this is a story about dying, from which I hope you can learn about living.

CHAPTER ONE

IN MY SECOND year of medical school I was sent out to a hospital in Bethlehem, Pennsylvania, an old steel town that had bottomed out in the nineties but had since bounced back into a vibrant, small community. I could relate. I had also gone through my own dark valley—losing my mother to cancer six years prior—and now I felt like I had climbed up and out onto the other side. My mom's death had inspired me to go into medicine in the first place; I had dreamed of helping patients like her, and I yearned to take revenge on her disease.

Picture me as a warrior in the battle against cancer, training so I could lay waste to the so-called emperor of all maladies, the king of terror. Picture me sharpening my tools and arming for war, stoic and full of wrath.

But first picture me on my obstetrics rotation, and absolutely terrified. On this particular day, I felt less like a warrior than like an actor. I had to keep rehearsing over and over in my head what I needed to do. I reviewed my steps, practiced my lines, worked through my checklist, and tried to remember how to play doctor. It really did feel like I was about to go onstage. The hospital room curtains had been thrust open, and the sun was streaming in, throwing a heavenly kind of spotlight on the first-time parents and all over the blue covering the nurse had just put down. Though both prospective parents were beaming with excitement, the mother's forehead glistened with sweat; I'm sure mine did too.

This husband-and-wife team were in their late twenties, which made them older than I was. It crossed my mind that Caitlin, then my girlfriend of three years, and I could find ourselves in this very same position soon enough, and that was a happy, calming thought. But perhaps I looked even more nervous than I thought I did, because the father asked, "This isn't your first time, is it?"

A scary thing about medicine is that everything in it has a first—every drug has a first patient, every surgeon has a first surgery, every method has a first try—and my life at the time was dominated, daily, by first times and new challenges.

But no, I assured this father-to-be I'd done this before. What I didn't say was: *once* before.

Then I was in position. My second Red Bull of the morning had kicked in, and I was ready.

As I cycled through the stages of labor in my mind, I was interrupted by the first sign of the baby—his head.

Don't drop it, Dave. Don't drop it, Dave. Don't drop it, Dave.

And that was that. I guided the baby safely into the world (it's actually easier than you might think), and I watched him take his first full breath of life. A profound sense of purpose spread through my body, into my limbs, and overwhelmed my senses so that I couldn't even notice the smell of feces and blood that attends every delivery. It didn't look like it did in movies. There was a lot more winging it, a lot more fear, a lot more relief.

There would be many times, later on, when I would remember that baby I delivered. What I did wasn't heroic or complicated or extraordinary by any measure. It was routine. But I had helped new life take flight and that was extraordinary. Too often hospital medicine isn't about new life—when doctors, nurses, and patients are assembled in a room, the reason is usually dire.

My first rotation working in a hospital where I could see this firsthand had been in January 2010, only a few months before my Bethlehem (Pennsylvania) baby. After four years of pre-med, a master's degree, and a year and a half of medical school coursework, it was finally time to apply my medical knowledge in situ. No more shadowing, no more observing. I might actually help save lives. I got about three hours of sleep the night before my first day—I couldn't remember being that amped up since my days of playing football. It was below freezing and before dawn when I got up to go to the hospital, but my adrenaline practically carried me there. I'd walked through the same entrance and atrium of the Hospital of the University of Pennsylvania many times before, but today it was totally different. The floors shone brighter. It was larger—or I was smaller. I smiled and waved at the security guards, who met my glee with dutiful reciprocity. They had likely seen dozens of glowing medical students that morning. Each of us, of course, dreaming that we'd be cracking cases and helping patients today like in an episode of *House*.

My first stop was the psychiatry resident call room, where I was supposed to meet up with what's called the psychiatry consult service. Basically our job would be to visit patients throughout the hospital whose treating physicians had decided they could benefit from additional psychiatric assistance. Some patients were simply delirious after surgery, but others had said they wanted to hurt themselves, or other people.

Psychiatry wasn't what I really wanted to be ultimately doing—all I could think about doing was fighting cancer—but I was eager to begin my clinical career on a good note. So I attacked the day with egregious enthusiasm. I greeted a woman a few years older than I—one of the residents—who was already engaged deeply in something on her computer screen. I extended my hand, introduced myself, and announced—unnecessarily—that this was my first rotation.

Then, as now, I was terrible at masking my mood. It has always been so achingly obvious. The resident could probably *smell* the nervousness on me.

Another medical student came in after me. Well, as I soon learned, he wasn't exactly a medical student, even though our role there in the consult service would be the same. He was already an oral surgeon; he'd already completed dental school *and* dental residency. He was now coming back to undertake a few medical school rotations that are mandatory to practice as an oral surgeon. I was competing against someone in his eighth year of medical training.

And—yes—it was a competition. We were both dressed like the plebs we were: in the same short white coats, just barely reaching our waists. This set us apart (as it was intended to do). The attending physician and other resident both arrived resplendent in coats that nearly reached the floor. My legs never felt so naked. Especially because Oral Surgeon over there actually could have worn the longer coat if he'd really wanted to. He'd already earned it. He'd already made his way through the gauntlet. Becoming a physician requires first acing premed courses in undergraduate, and then grinding through four years of medical school. That's step one. After that, you *technically* get your long coat, but you still need to complete residency and possibly fellowship training, which can last from three to more than twelve years—depending on specialty—before you can finally practice on your own as an attending. I still had a long way to go. But a first day was a first step.

Our morning greetings and introductions (and my private ruminations) were interrupted by the beeps of a pager. Our first mission of the day. We rushed down the hall in order of rank—Oral Surgeon and I took up the rear.

When we got to the patient's room, a lump immediately rose in my throat. The room was dark. The patient was very sick. His cheeks were swollen from the corticosteroid treatments he'd been on, which reminded me of the way my mom had looked when being treated (also with corticosteroids) for her cancer. Her swollen cheeks had exaggerated her smile. The memory was bittersweet. I knew that I was going to struggle if I constantly thought of my mother. But I couldn't shut those memories out. I didn't want to—remembering her smile with those big cheeks made me smile.

This patient wasn't just sick; he was critically ill, and our goal was to evaluate whether or not he had the capacity to make medical decisions for himself. A woman sat beside the bed, holding the patient's hand. His wife, we soon learned. Tears dripped down her face, untouched, and eventually made their way down between her hands, where she'd gathered some blanket. A small piece of comfort, now also damp with her sadness. The patient was confused, and he struggled to answer our questions on the mental status exam.

"Where are we?"

"I'm in New . . ."

We were in Philadelphia.

"What year is it?"

"Nineteen seventy-seven."

It was 2010.

We huddled outside the room, but the decision wasn't difficult and the discussion was brief. The patient didn't have capacity to make his own medical decisions; his wife should make them for him.

Of course, medicine isn't always so binary. It's not just life or death, joy or despair. A middle ground exists where joy is possible in the face of death.

My time as a member of the psychiatry consult service would be distinguished neither by duration nor by any particular talent.

That is to say: When my two weeks on psychiatry consult were up, I happily transferred to working on the inpatient psychiatric ward, a locked unit in Pennsylvania Hospital. It was an intimidating place for a young doctor in training, a place for patients on the edge: struggling with depression, bipolar disorder, schizophrenia, and suicidality. Though this rotation was a necessary step toward becoming a doctor, I didn't expect it to actually hone any future cancer-fighting skills.

My first patient there was George. Aged fifty-two, divorced, tall with broad shoulders, George had been diagnosed with glioblastoma, an aggressive brain cancer—the worst kind, and the kind my mom had had. One side of his face drooped, and he walked with a limp. But that's not why he was in the hospital. He was in the psychiatric ward for depression and his stated wish to commit suicide. Just that week he'd been told he had two months to live.

My resident told me that George had not wanted to talk to anyone since he arrived and that he had stayed in his room almost all day, every day. She asked me to perform a mental status exam on him to round out his admission paperwork. Despite having a rapidly growing brain tumor, he scored a perfect 30 out of 30. Most of the patients that I evaluated who didn't have tumors growing in their brains scored around 25.

He was anything but dour when I showed him the results.

"I aced it, Doc! Do I get anything special for it?"

"I know. Way to go. Let me get back to you on your prize." I grinned.

He walked away with more confidence than when he'd come in. It was visible even in his stride, in his carriage. His limp looked more like a strut.

But later that day, I saw him lying in his bed without the TV on. He was just staring at the wall. It seemed that the high I'd helped him get to with the test score was only temporary. *Okay, even if it was only temporary, it could be repeated.* There wasn't any reason I couldn't help him strut again. If that was the best we could hope for, it seemed eminently worth trying.

I searched the Internet to find a new mental status exam that I could administer. This time he scored 28 out of 30, nearly as good as before, and well above the normal threshold of 25. Again, George smiled from ear to ear. The next morning, I didn't see him lying in bed—I found him at the nurses' station, bragging to all who would listen about how well he'd done on the two previous tests.

I ended up giving George a mental status exam each afternoon he was in the hospital. They weren't necessary for his care and none of them ever went in his chart, but that was hardly the point. George's transformation from suicidal to upbeat had turned a routine piece of hospital paperwork into a joyful routine for both of us. In time, it led to something more.

One part of the mental status exam instructs the patient to write any sentence he wants to on a piece of paper. Each time, George would write something about his daughter, Ashley. On Monday he wrote "I love Ashley." On Tuesday: "It was Ashley's birthday Saturday." On Wednesday he wrote "I miss Ashley." On Thursday: "I love Ashley!" The pattern was clear: Ashley was important to him. So I asked him about her. I learned that he hadn't talked with her in a while but that he left voicemails with her every day. I am not naïve: I knew the situation was much more complicated than I could appreciate. I knew that estrangement has many causes, and many contributors. But at the same time, sitting in the psychiatric ward, watching a man spend his last days writing simple notes to his daughter that she would never see and leaving voicemails that she would not return—it wasn't too complicated to untangle. I asked George if I could call Ashley simply to tell her how well he was doing, about his great tests and the notes, and about what it was like for me when my mom had brain cancer. He agreed. So I called and left her my own voicemail.

The next day I saw George and asked him how he was doing. "I'm doing great! Ashley called last night!"

When I rounded the corner, out of his sight, I gave a fist pump. This was the first time that I may have really helped one of my patients. And it wasn't even some complicated procedure or coup of surgical dexterity. I hadn't uncovered a medical mystery. I simply let my hope and desire for George to be happy during his final days direct my actions. George and I had gotten to a breakthrough by doing some paperwork. That's all it was. The things that sustain us need not be anything more.

While I had witnessed pure joy for the new parents and devastating despair for the incapacitated patient and his wife, I actually helped to bring about joy in the face of sadness for George.

And it felt so good. I wanted more.

Luckily for me, this phase of medical training is pretty much set up to give you more, and more, and more, and more. More than you can ever really handle.

CHAPTER TWO

I SHOULD HAVE been too tired to do much of anything outside the hospital, but the endless hours and high pressure were actually energizing for me and pumped me up to take on more. In between grueling rotations and long hours on the wards, my best friends from medical school and I would steal time to hit the gym. Between exercises, we practiced what we called dynamic rest—we grumbled about rotations, hospital staff, and, for me in the first weeks, Oral Surgeon.

Since I'm a shell of my former self today, I don't feel like it's bragging for me to share that I could bench-press 375 pounds back then. My friends started calling me the Beast. Even as a Division I college football player, I had never been more Beastly.

One night, a group of my friends were watching a Phillies game in my apartment while I studied in my room. I came out for a study break just as Ryan Howard was up to bat. At the time, he was one of the top power hitters in Major League Baseball. The commentator said that Howard could bench-press 350 pounds. My friend Aaron looked at me and said, "Howard's using his three-hundred-fifty-pound bench press to hit homers. What are you using your bench press for? Holding back the skin during surgery?" Everyone laughed. Perhaps sensing that my laughter was a little forced, Aaron emailed me the next day with a link to a bench-pressing contest in Stanardsville, Virginia, with the words "Put that bench press to use." I'm still not sure if he was entirely serious, but I took him up on the challenge: A few weeks later, nine of us packed into two cars to drive five hours from Philadelphia to Stanardsville, a town of about five hundred residents. I would be the only one competing, but my friends were willing to squander their precious downtime to show their support. Luckily for me, this particular league required participants to give a same-day urine sample, so I wouldn't be competing against anyone using illegal performance enhancers. All I took were my requisite three Red Bulls—totally legal.

I wasn't hitting home runs for the Phillies, but I did win the bench-pressing contest that year for my weight class in Stanardsville. I missed the state record by five pounds. My friends cheered "Beast! Beast!" We celebrated hard that night.

Maybe my bench-press adventures prove what some who know me would tell you: I'm a bit of a glutton for punishment. Which may be one reason that the constant demands of being a young doctor in training suited me perfectly. It felt like the more that was asked from me, the more I was able to put into everything I did, both in work and in play. Seeing what I could do to help people like George pushed me to focus on everything else I could do. It felt like I was finally discovering potential I had buried or put into cold storage during my first couple years of medical school.

It was an old, good feeling. What had always truly helped me the most, back in school, back on the field, was that I could *focus* better and work harder than anyone. It's the only way I ever got to excel in football; I played quarterback at Georgetown very much despite my God-given lack of foot speed.

After struggling following my mom's death, I was back up. I had the bull by the horns. I was healthy, I was thriving. I was the Virginia bench-pressing champion in my weight class, and I had a wonderful girlfriend, Caitlin, who had been a pillar of strength and support for me while I coped with my mother's death and was now—even at a distance (she was living in Raleigh, North Carolina, finishing up her final year of college)—every bit as supportive of my drive to become a doctor. And here I was making strides toward one day defeating the disease that had killed my mother. I felt like I was conquering the world.

But I was leaving worlds behind.

One night, just a couple weeks after Stanardsville, I was studying for my neurology rotation—flash card after flash card after flash card—when my phone rang. It was Caitlin. We traveled between Philadelphia and Raleigh nearly every other weekend to see each other and had just spent a long holiday weekend together. It occurred to me that maybe she'd just come from a Fajgenbaum family dinner—she went to these even when I wasn't in Raleigh to join them—and was calling to fill me in on family happenings. Or maybe she'd just come home from work and had something funny to share—when she wasn't in class, she worked at my sister's clothing store or babysat my three-year-old niece, Anne Marie. No matter the topic, these calls always seemed to help me feel good.

Immediately, this one felt different.

"Hey," she said, "we need to talk." Even though she'd said only five words, she sounded uncharacteristically sad and anxious. Now I wondered if she'd gotten bad news at work, had something go wrong in class, or if something had happened to her parents or brother, all of whom I cared deeply for. Then eight more words that felled me: "I think we need to take a break."

It was a stunning blow. In no iteration of my life plan was Caitlin not there. Didn't she know that? Had I neglected to tell her? I needed her by my side. I thought, I assumed, she knew that and wanted me by her side too. I was at a loss for words.

So, eventually and lamely, I just said, "Okay." Then there was a long pause.

It strikes me now that my reluctance to probe further and ask *why* was because I already knew but didn't want to hear it. My torpedo-like focus, that thing that had helped me in so many ways and would help me so much in the future, was rarely directed at Caitlin.

So, she filled the strange silence herself. "I think we need a break because you're just not making me a priority."

I knew what she was saying, but I couldn't help thinking: *You knew all of this. You knew what I had to do, and what we were getting into. We have made it work for three years. We managed to keep this relationship alive—and have some of the happiest times of our lives together—despite time and geographic constraints: while I was at Georgetown and you were four hours away in Raleigh. I went away for a whole year to get a master's in England and I worked my tail off to complete it in less than one year so I could return to the States to be closer to you. I've been seven hours away at medical school for two years already. I've had competing priorities all along, but you've always been near the top of my list. Don't you know that? Why now? Why didn't you bring this up when we were together last week? Why don't you want to be together anymore?*

But I was too stunned to say any of that or even protest; I let the silence stretch out, which only seemed to galvanize her to end things. My utter surprise and speechlessness also represented our poor communication, which was likely a factor underlying this breakup in the first place. Somehow, we hung up the phone.

Then, I broke my silence. "Is that it? Should I fight for us?" I said out loud. I allowed myself to indulge a kind of fairy-tale belief that everything would work out, that if this was "meant to be," we'd find our way back to each other. Now clearly wasn't the right time or at least that's what I was telling myself to dampen the pain. Young, healthy, and largely blindsided, I thought that we had all the time in the world to work this out. I didn't need to act. I could just wait and see.

After the shock of it set in, I responded to our breakup the same way that had gotten me into this mess. I became even more focused. I studied harder. I worked longer hours in the hospital. I worked out and became even more Beastly. I did not want to stand still long enough to face what had happened. If I ran hard enough, I could outrun the pain.

Two months later, Caitlin made it impossible to keep running from her. She was visiting her parents in Philadelphia and asked me to go out to dinner. Afterward, she told me she was ready for us to get back together if I was willing to make her a priority again. I was still hurt and living in a mindset that if it was meant to be, it would work out when the moment was right. My hyperfocusing over the last few months had prevented me from recognizing the feelings I still had for her. I turned her down. We had time, so I refocused on everything else.

But there was only so much I could deny, rationalize, or compartmentalize. Life—and death—kept marching on, oblivious to my need to bury my head in the sand.

A week later, a thin but healthy-looking woman in her sixties came into the emergency room with classic symptoms of a stroke. I was with the resident on the stroke service that morning when we got the page. We ran down the halls to the ER— and we really ran. The patient's speech didn't make any sense, and the right side of her body was paralyzed. We rushed her into the CT scanner.

It was dire. The resident spoke to the woman and her husband: "There's a medication that could possibly reverse some of the symptoms if given soon after onset. But there are serious potential side effects, risks you would be taking with its administration." She explained what the risks were. But the message was clear: We had to move quickly if we were going to move at all. And there were huge implications to this decision.

We stepped out of the room to give the husband and wife the privacy to decide what they wanted to do. When the husband emerged and told us they wanted to move forward with the treatment, we jumped into action to get the infusion started.

I sat beside the patient's bed, monitoring her for any signs of improvement. Actually—I wasn't just monitoring; I was hoping and praying. That first minute of assessment felt like an eternity. And then she began to change. But not for the better. Instead, she got worse, rapidly. Her speech disintegrated more. She became unintelligible. She was experiencing a rare, but well understood, complication of the treatment: an intracranial hemorrhage or brain bleed. She began to struggle to breathe. We immediately stopped the treatment and did everything we could to keep her alive, including tilting the bed all the way upright, starting new medications, consulting with neurosurgery about performing an emergency craniotomy, and doing a lot of praying and hoping. Despite our best efforts, she died within three hours. This outcome was an uncommon but known risk, and we had informed her and her husband of it, but that didn't make it any easier.

I was twenty-five years old and had lost "my" first patient. I left the room in tears.

That the statement "There was nothing we could do" is a cliché does not diminish its truth; it only makes the statement feel utterly outmatched by the reality it is supposed to convey. There was nothing more we could do to save her once she experienced the treatment's rare complication. But if we hadn't administered the drug to try to cure her in the first place, she may have survived, though with significant mental and physical disabilities. It was the most bitter possible lesson for someone like me, someone who had made *doing* the center of his life until it had expanded to push everything else out.

I grew up a Catholic, and a hopeful one. I believed in the power of medicine, and the power of prayer to augment that medicine. An underpinning condition for my work ethic was a faith that if I did the right thing, and did it hard enough, the "right thing" would eventually win out. In my mind, the war would always be won before the first battle. If I hit the weight room and practice fields hard enough in the winter and spring, I knew that I could win the starting position and have success on game days in the fall. You get what you deserve. So far in my life, it had been mostly true.

My mother's death had opened my eyes to the possibility that this wasn't true. Medical school lectures on genetics, health, and disease made this more clear. But it was in this moment that I realized—shockingly suddenly, as perhaps it is for most people when the penny finally drops—that life wasn't fair. Did this woman deserve to have an exceedingly rare and lethal drug reaction? Well, if everything happens for a reason, then maybe it was meant to teach her husband a valuable lesson that he couldn't have learned without bearing witness to her death. I didn't really buy that. And then my mind—unleashed by this sadness—started to cast around for other examples of its faulty assumptions: What about the people who die due to genetic alterations that occur completely randomly at conception? Had those lethal mutations been divinely organized to teach some kind of lesson to the grieving families left behind? What about babies who die alone in orphanages? Who learns a lesson in their deaths? Sparked by this one senseless emergency room death, I saw in a flash that I couldn't expect to be blessed with good outcomes just because I worked hard, made good decisions, and did the most I could do to help others. The bubble burst. Comeuppance! Everything that happens in life may not always be for the best. Perhaps this realization was well overdue. Somewhere in the back of my mind I understood there was a lesson here to be learned about my relationship with Caitlin. I held that thought at bay.

CHAPTER THREE

TECHNICALLY I'M DISABLED. As a kid I was diagnosed with the hyperfocus variant of attention deficit/hyperactivity disorder. This helps explain how, even from a young age, I could do things like work out for hours or sit and watch game film on my opponents well after my teammates had lost interest.

Don't get me wrong—it's not a superpower. It gets in the way of being able to move from one task to another. Like when you are in a constant state of missing the forest for the trees: When you hyperfocus, one tree can become very, very, very, very interesting.

Ultimately, making sure that what's interesting is also worthy and regimenting every minute into my calendar was the way I made my ADHD work for me (most of the time). My parents modeled what a life with the right priorities can look like; I borrowed, internalized, and used their strategies, and my iCal calendar took me the rest of the way.

I grew up in Raleigh, North Carolina. My parents had immigrated to the United States from the Caribbean island of

Trinidad so that my dad could go to college and then medical school. After medical school, they moved to North Carolina so my dad could complete a rigorous orthopedic surgery residency while my mother stayed home to raise Gena, Lisa, and me. I think it was from my mom that I most directly inherited my work ethic. She was a faithful Catholic and put her faith into action for our family and in the community. She worked tirelessly to make sure my dad, sisters, and I received the support we needed and learned critical life lessons. She often took me on trips to deliver food to elderly church members during the week. On weekends, we would go on charity walks, or work in soup kitchens, or volunteer at the North Carolina Special Olympics. Helping other people—being present for them—made her tick. It wasn't just a nice thing to do. She believed it was her responsibility, and she loved it.

My dad, the formidable orthopedic surgeon, played against type. He's the most extroverted person I've ever met. He's also full of opinions and stories—both of which he absolutely will share with you, whether or not you ask for them (or you've heard them before). It was from him that I absorbed a belief in education as the surest way to overcome barriers, something he learned from his own father, who lost his entire family in the Holocaust. My grandfather made a life for himself in Trinidad after the war, despite not being able to speak a word of English when he arrived there. He married my Guyanese grandmother, whose family had been in Latin America for generations, though she had roots from all over the world, including sub-Saharan West Africa. My mother's family had immigrated to Trinidad from Europe generations before. My lineage is like Trinidad itself: a melting pot of culture, skin tone, and religion; I have one Jewish grandparent and three Catholic grandparents.

My dad's expectations for me and my sisters were very high: He wanted us to find a calling and to succeed as he had done. How could I not gravitate toward orthopedic surgery? I witnessed a parade of wheelchairs enter my dad's office and then later, after surgery and his follow-up care, I saw people leave on their own two feet. His patients got better, all of them, no matter how complex the problem.

But I also knew that medicine took up almost all of his time. He always seemed to be working. He left before I woke up and got home only in time for a late dinner. He was gone most weekends too, though to his credit he somehow never missed a single one of my football games. I guess his sideline attendance sent a message too: Success as a father was a priority as well.

So while I idly puzzled over how I could be a miracle worker (in medicine) and yet still have time for the family I imagined I'd have someday, I focused my laser attention on succeeding in football.

I began dreaming about playing quarterback for a Division I college team when I was seven years old. And by dreaming I don't mean like at night; I mean every day, all day, all I thought about was football. Remember: hyperfocus. My dad was the doctor for the NC State Wolfpack football team, and I got to accompany him into the locker room and onto the sidelines for home games. Most games drew tens of thousands of fans, a fact that blew me away every time. And I was in awe of the size, speed, and tenacity of the players; they were like gods to me.

By the time I got to middle school, I began to realize that natural skills and speed were not on my side. If I was really going to excel on the field, I needed to improve. A lot. I didn't have the sheer natural talent that I already saw expressing itself in some of my teammates. I needed more skills, more athleticism, more everything. So I started training for hours every day. I worked out during study halls, as well as every morning or afternoon. I read books on exercise science and nutrition, and spent hours watching game film of myself and my opponents. I never got to be the fastest kid on the field, but I bet I had more charts on my walls than any thirteen-year-old in the country:

progress markers for forty-yard dashes, mile times, throwing accuracy, and throwing distance. I trained hard, and I kept the receipts. I could see my investments paying off on the charts and on the field. I realized that even if none of us has control over the skills or talents we're born with, we all have complete control over how hard we work.

With my dad gone most of the time, and my sisters five and seven years older than I, my mother was in many ways my closest friend and ally. We even tossed the football together. But as my strength began to develop, I started throwing it too hard for her to catch. Eager to find a workaround, she created a system that would allow us to be together and her to help: She set up and stood near targets at the top of a hill behind our house, and she'd roll the ball back down to me after I tried to hit them. She never pushed me to play football. In fact, she would have preferred if I hadn't played because she was so worried about me getting injured. But she knew I loved it and she wanted to support me, even if it involved rolling balls down a hill for hours. We loved and lived the motto "Practice does not make perfect. Only perfect practice makes perfect."

My high school football coach, Ned Gonet, saw my work ethic and upped the ante. He had played fullback at Duke and then in the NFL and was a legend in North Carolina football, a terror on the practice field. He was on my tail from day one. If I wasn't perfect, he yelled at me. If I was perfect, he yelled at me for not having been perfect before. His pursuit of improvement was relentless, and it shaped how I felt about success from the beginning: It wasn't ever some discrete position, some mark on the wall that we worked to reach. If that was all success was, we could reach it and then the work would be over. Ned taught me that success has to be dynamic—mine is and was different from that of the guy next to me, and it was also different from day to day. Training to be better than the next guy or the next team wasn't the point; training to be the best possible was the point.

When you reach a goal: push the goal back. In this context, criticism isn't punishment; it's the pull of the next goal, already calling out your name.

Not that hard work *guaranteed* anything; I learned that the hard way. When I led my high school team to the state championship in my junior year, and lost, I immediately set my sights on winning the next year. Colleges had already been recruiting me, and I knew that football was as much a part of my future as it was my present. Then both of those timelines collapsed simultaneously. On the first scrimmage of my senior year, my collarbone snapped into three fragments. My dad looked at the X-rays and told me, flatly, that I would never play football again. Then he got to work. He operated on me the next day. Luckily he's a better surgeon than he is a fortune-teller, and I was able to rejoin the team and take on the starting quarterback role by midseason. We actually made it back to the championship. A late fourth-quarter drive that I could have only dreamed of put us in the lead with a few minutes remaining. And then the magic ran out. We lost, again. There would be no fairy-dusted finale for me or my team.

The championship loss was only part of my disappointment. After my injury, many of the colleges that had been recruiting me pulled back, understandably, and my dream of Division I football recalibrated from those images of my youth—the bright lights of the Atlantic Coast Conference, tens of thousands of fans, and nationally televised games—to the more academically focused confines of the Patriot and Ivy Leagues. I chose Georgetown. My opponents would include the Bears of Brown University, the Big Red of Cornell, and the Leopards of Lafayette. Academic All-Stars and future corporate executives up and down the depth chart. Big time for fans of highly strategic, disciplined football. So, while Georgetown was not a perennial football powerhouse, it was still Division I and it turned out to be a perfect fit. It gave me the opportunity to play football at a high level and emphasized the kind of service that my mother's example had stamped into me as important. It also demanded the kind of academic excellence that my father valued. I would be a Hoya through and through.

When my parents drove me up to Washington, D.C., for my freshman year, my dad was in high spirits, as usual, but my mother was unusually quiet. When I had a moment alone with her I asked what she was feeling, assuming she was sad about seeing her youngest leave the proverbial nest. Instead, she said she'd been having really bad headaches for a while, and she was confused about what was going on. But I continued—as eighteen-year-olds will do—to think her feelings were all about me. I told her it was likely stress related and not to worry about me. I'd be okay.

Before my parents headed home, we all paid a visit to my new football coach. As we were leaving his office, a group of older players happened to be walking by. I won't soon forget the awkward moment: While my mom supportively rubbed my back, my dad shook the coach's hand and said, pleadingly, "Coach—take care of my baby boy."

The upperclassmen burst out laughing. And before the first day of class, I'd received my nickname, Davey Boy.

I made better use of my next opportunity to make a first impression. A week later, we played our first seven-on-seven scrimmage, against Howard University, and I was quarterback. Five touchdowns later—and no interceptions—we rolled. I called home to tell my parents all about it. When my dad answered, I regaled him with the play-by-play, with all of my joy. He was silent. Eventually he spoke.

"Your mom has brain cancer." And although he didn't need to say it, he went on. "You need to come home."

On the plane ride back to North Carolina—finally alone with my thoughts—eighteen years of memories swirled through my mind. My mother's silhouette standing at the top of the hill behind my house. Sitting in church beside me. Staying up late with me while I studied for exams. Feeding people, nurturing them, helping strangers. Doing.

When I arrived at Duke's Brain Tumor Center, she'd already been taken into the operating room to remove as much of the tumor as possible. My father and sisters and I sat in the waiting room together, and we talked about the road ahead below a sign on the wall that said AT DUKE, THERE IS HOPE. The sign was comforting, but we understood that the complexity of brain surgery meant that survival wasn't the only outcome to think about—we wondered if she'd be the same person after a portion of her brain had been removed. We wondered if she'd be able to speak. We wondered if she'd remember who we were. After we were told that the surgery had gone as planned and were at last allowed to see her, I huddled my family in the hallway and urged them not to cry in front of her. My logic was that if we were crying, Mom would worry about us, and that was precisely what she didn't need to do at this critical time.

No one spoke as we approached her bed. When she could see us, she pointed to her head, bandaged and attached to tubes and beepers. "Chiquita Banana Lady," she said, smiling. We all laughed and cried tears of joy. We still had our mom. We had hope.

The next day, when the doctors informed us that her tumor was a grade 4 glioblastoma, I told my sisters, "At least it's not grade five." I later learned that there is no grade 5; 4 is the worst. I didn't ask about the average survival for someone like my mom—I asked about the *longest* that a patient with a grade 4 glioblastoma had ever lived. I was looking for any bit of hope to grab on to, even imaginary scraps and false leads. One of the doctors said, "I'm aware of someone living five years." So, as far as I was concerned, that meant we had at least five years and one day to spend with Mom. Doing may have been her default mode, but she also instilled in me a belief that anything is possible with prayer. If anyone deserved a miracle, it was her. So I prayed.

I didn't want to go back to Georgetown, but my mom was adamant. She wanted me to pursue the dream I had been chasing since I was a child. I agreed to return to school after my sisters agreed to move home from New York City, where they had been living since college, and we all promised to see one another almost every weekend.

My mother had lived the kind of life that meant she'd have lots of people adding her to their intercessions. One weekend that I was home I went to our pharmacy to pick up her chemotherapy prescriptions. The cashier, whose name tag told me she was named Kim, broke into tears when she learned whom I was picking up for. Apparently, my mom had frequently spent hours with her, talking through challenges that Kim was facing in her life. I knew what Kim was feeling. The role reversal was painful.

Over the next few months I shuttled back and forth between Georgetown and home, and my family drove up to Georgetown for home games. I asked to be taken off the travel squad so I could go home during away games, a decision that I never could have imagined making just a couple months earlier but that was perfectly clear and easy at the time. When I was on campus, I felt completely alone. It's not that I didn't have great friends. But I didn't have anyone to turn to who really understood, firsthand, what I was going through. As we fell into the rhythm of treatments and MRIs and hoping for good news, I began to appreciate the profound impact my mom's doctors were having on her life, and on ours. My hyperfocus started to shift targets. Medical school had always been in the back of my mind, but now it was not orthopedics that was beckoning. I began to dream of helping patients in the way my mom's doctors were so clearly trying to help her.

But there was only so much they could do. Her memory began to deteriorate. Well—her short-term memory, anyway.

She might forget to turn off the faucet after washing her hands, but when we watched home videos together she remembered all the moments relived on the screen. And then some: She sometimes filled in gaps in the footage or gave us the backstory to the scene. Many of these stories were totally new to me, and I was grateful and eager to hear them from her perspective. I spent the entire summer after my freshman year with my mom. We went to physical therapy, radiation appointments, doctors' visits, and church together. We prayed often and hoped constantly. Even after an MRI showed that her cancer had returned despite the intensive treatments and was now inoperable, my mom said it had been the "best year ever" because our family had spent so much time together. Despite the chemo, despite the cancer, despite the radiation. She was dying with joy.

I didn't have the words yet, but now that I've gone through some of what my mother went through during her last year, I realize that she wasn't just a kind and generous person; she was someone with a ferociously powerful will. I now see that "will" is that extra fight that emerges when there seems to be no more hope.

One of the greatest signs of a strong will is being able to find a silver lining while fighting in the midst of the storm. The kind of willpower that my mother showed me was something else though. She didn't just look for silver linings. She created her own silver linings. That last year really was a joyful time. That sounds almost impossible. It wasn't. Her attitude toward that year was executive and authorial: She decided there would be good memories for her family after she was gone, and then she set about making them happen. For her and for us.

A simple trip to the grocery store immediately comes to mind. The cancer had nearly completely paralyzed the right side of her body, so walking was quite difficult for her. But she could lean on me until we got inside the store, and then she decided to use their motorized cart. But she could squeeze only one handle, so the cart went in circles. I thought she was going to cry—I would have—but when the cart began to circle back toward me, I saw that she had a big smile on her face. And she just kept doing circles while we laughed together. I'll never walk past one of those carts without thinking of her and that laughter. She created that silver lining and she gave it to me that day. She showed me that I didn't need to hope for a miracle to happen or for someone else to make things better for me or someone I loved—I could grab it by the handle and make it happen myself.

CHAPTER FOUR

I STRUGGLED WITH returning to school in the fall for my sophomore year, so I traveled home every weekend to spend time with my mom. A few months later—in October 2004—we had our final visit and conversation. She worried about whether I'd be okay. I told her that I would and that I'd create a group in her memory to help other grieving college students—something I had never thought of before that moment. Then, I added that I would name it AMF—after her initials, Anne Marie Fajgenbaum—and it would be her work, her life living on through me.

Her words at that point were limited. She smiled and responded, "Unconditional love." She passed away two weeks later. I was nineteen.

I was impaled by my mother's death. There's no other word for it. How could this happen? She was the hardest-working, kindest, and most giving person I had ever met. She ate exquisitely healthfully, exercised daily, and didn't smoke or drink. She made her life all about helping others. Why would God do this to my mom? If He was truly in control, why would He choose to take her? Her diagnosis and death introduced the first cracks in my foundation and my belief in order and hope.

A few weeks later, I found a scrap of paper in my mother's purse. It was a clipping from a newspaper, yellowed, framed in Scotch tape, and bearing the unmistakable signs of having been a frequently consulted source of inspiration. It was only a fragment, but I was able to make out that it was from a story about Pope John Paul II and a trip he made to Cuba in 1998. It included a quotation from his speech:

> Dear young people, whether you are believers or not, accept the call to be virtuous. This means being strong within, having a big heart, being rich in the highest sentiments, bold in the truth, courageous in freedom, constant in responsibility, generous in love, invincible in hope.

Inspired by these words, I knew what I needed to do. I returned to Georgetown on a mission. I formally founded AMF, which I decided would now also stand for Ailing Mothers & Fathers. It included a peer grief support group and community service projects in honor of deceased parents. I quickly learned that many other students—even a close friend of mine, Kate— were also grieving, but we all felt alone because no one talked about it. We soon opened it up to any students coping with the illness or death of a loved one and changed the meaning of AMF again, this time to Actively Moving Forward, to reflect our inclusivity. Each struggling student who shared his or her story of loneliness and lack of support on campus motivated me to work harder. Every time that I was sad about my mom's death, I channeled more energy into AMF. My high school best friend, Ben, impelled by his own grief following the death of my mom— who had been like a mother to him—started another chapter of

AMF at the University of North Carolina. By the time the tenth student contacted me about starting a chapter of AMF on another campus, Ben and I decided to turn AMF into a national nonprofit organization. During my last two years at Georgetown, and for many years thereafter, I would work twenty to forty hours a week as the unpaid executive director for AMF and start chapters of the group on college campuses across the country.

There was nothing—nothing—inherently "positive" about my mother dying the way she did. She willed positivity into that last year. I borrowed some of that willpower she left behind to will AMF into existence. It's helped support thousands of grieving kids all over the country. It's a silver lining, no doubt. It didn't exist before I put it there.

My work ethic seemed to finally find full expression when mixed with a sense of purpose beyond the end zone. Football slipped down my list of priorities as I focused on AMF's nationwide spread. Medicine shot up. I wanted to become an oncologist to take on cancer. I wanted revenge.

During my senior year I received a scholarship to complete a master's at the University of Oxford, focused on cancer prevention. After that, or so my plan went, I would be fully prepared to start med school and become a warrior against cancer in earnest. I was excited to begin this next stage, and I prepared to go over to England like I was getting ready to go to boot camp. And then, as plans do, this one got upended a bit. I met Caitlin at a bar in Raleigh while I was home visiting my family over winter break.

It turned out that we had both gone to Ravenscroft High School in Raleigh, though because she was two and a half years younger than I and had transferred there just six months before I graduated, we never actually met. After high school she had gone on to study at Meredith College in Raleigh, where, incidentally, my mom had enrolled in her late forties and completed half of her requirements for a college degree before cancer derailed her plans.

We may not have met while in high school, but Caitlin remembers the first time our paths crossed. It was at a high school basketball game. She noticed that a fan for the other team was wearing a football jersey with FAGENBAUM printed on the back. She didn't think much of it; she didn't know whom the shirt was even referring to. But then she saw a Ravenscroft student run to the other side of the court and up into the visitor stands. He ripped the jersey right down the middle before security ushered him out of the arena to jeers and boos from the other team's fans.

That jersey ripper was me! The taunt on that jersey wasn't about basketball; it was a holdover of resentment from our football rivalry.

After the game, when Caitlin told her mom what happened, her mom told her that she couldn't go to any more basketball games and warned her to stay away from that Fajgenbaum boy.

Here we were four years later.

When I spotted her at the bar, I immediately remembered her. We had a number of friends in common but had never actually met. She had sent me a Facebook friend request a few months before. And I had sent her a message that since we were now Facebook friends, which meant we must be very close friends (that's how it was in the 2000s), we should actually meet when I was in Raleigh next. When I got the courage to walk over to her at the bar, we hugged like we had known each other for years and were just catching up.

Which is, oddly, how it felt. I complained about my pre-med classes, and she told me all about her classes in fashion merchandising at Meredith. Though ordinarily I would have avoided invoking my mom and the follow-up questions that might take our first conversation in a sad or morbid direction, I told Caitlin about my mom's experience at Meredith and about her too-young and recent death. Nothing seemed off-limits.

My heart was thumping wildly. I got her, she got me. We could both feel it, but I made a real effort not to show my cards—I spent the next thirty minutes talking to other people so as not to let on my interest. But every time I turned to look at Caitlin while I was making my rounds, she was looking back at me. She was gorgeous, and her smile was beautiful. Trying to make Caitlin smile soon became a new target for my hyperfocus.

We began dating long distance during my final semester at Georgetown. Between me traveling down to Raleigh or her up to D.C., we managed to see each other almost every weekend. She also loved what I was doing through AMF and even started a chapter at Meredith College. She was our—and my—biggest cheerleader.

For the first time ever, I found someone who could get me to take a break from work. And I liked it. Caitlin also was one of the few people in my family or friend network who felt comfortable calling me out about a bad idea or something that I needed to improve upon. Who else would have told me that I had to cut the overly dramatic nods with pursed lips I made with each question during my first televised interview about AMF? I promised to work on my listening face.

Before I left for Oxford, we committed to making our relationship work despite the distance. My master's was supposed to be a two-year program, but I didn't want to be away from Caitlin for that long and I was also eager to get on with medical school and residency thereafter. One week into my program, I asked to meet with the program director and broached the subject of accelerating my studies. It wasn't an easy conversation. He warned that I'd need to perform two years' worth of full-time, graduate-level work to achieve the master's. I set out to do it in eight months.

I worked around the clock to meet my self-imposed deadline and also to lead AMF, which really began to gain traction and even national attention, from abroad. The *Today* show and *Read-*

er's Digest would run stories about our work that year, and the story of AMF's creation would be printed on the backs of 20 million bags of Cool Ranch Doritos in 2007 and 2008. College kids love Doritos, so those bags contributed to a surge of new chapters of AMF. But I was surprised to learn that awareness does not always translate into action or, in this case, donations. Millions of people saw those stories, hundreds of people emailed me to congratulate me on my work, but just a few donated to support it. Perhaps the publicity of iterative successes gives people the perception that the problem is solved or others are already on the case; it's difficult to express how hard it was to get that far, and how much more there still was to do. I also think that many assumed AMF must be receiving donations from other people and bursting with funds *because of* the coverage we were getting, so they chose not to donate themselves.

I did carve out some time to play quarterback for the Oxford Cavaliers (American) football team. It was a different level of competition than I was used to, but it was a familiar hobby and quenched my ever-present desire to be a part of a team. And, not inconsequentially, it was fun. I knew I needed that outlet in my life.

My time in Oxford also introduced me to the world of biomedical research. And what I saw alarmed me. Back when I had watched the doctors work together at Duke to treat my mother, all I saw was impressive coordination and cooperation among parts of a well-oiled machine. I just assumed that same kind of organization threaded up into research and out into all parts of the medical world, that everyone worked together in pursuit of a common goal: saving lives.

Instead, I started to realize there was a stunning lack of collaboration in many places, especially among cancer and cardiovascular disease prevention researchers. Though diet, physical inactivity, and smoking are the top three preventable risk factors for both diseases, researchers studied them in silos. They hardly worked across the aisle; they barely seemed to work with others even in their own specialties. For example, studies of the impact of risk factor modification on cancer prevention didn't track the impact on cardiovascular disease prevention. And vice versa. The chopped-up terrain was basically feudal: I saw a civil war battleground instead of a collection of people working to save lives by fighting together against the real enemy. My research dissertation concluded as much and suggested a more unified approach, whereby cancer prevention and cardiovascular disease prevention research would leverage findings from each other. It was a bit awkward to share with researchers, but most weren't too surprised by my findings.

Nonetheless, my hyperfocusing paid off. I met my eight-month goal and was overjoyed to go home to Caitlin and to begin medical school at the University of Pennsylvania on a full scholarship. I would continue to lead AMF full-time as an unpaid executive director during my first year and a half of medical school. I'd catch up on medical school lectures by watching videos of them sped up to 2.2 times the regular speed. There was no time to sleep, so I took caffeine pills and drank energy drinks to keep me awake.

In my mind, I was on a mission and I'd nearly gotten to the final stage.

In truth, I was pursuing my obsessions with reckless intensity. Whether or not I could keep it up soon became a moot issue.

CHAPTER FIVE

IN JULY 2010, I had six months of med school rotations under my belt, and I could look forward to two weeks of vacation. All I wanted to do was see my family: my dad; my sisters, Lisa and Gena; and Gena's daughter, Anne Marie, and husband, Chris. I couldn't wait to get home, and I rushed through the terminal in the Raleigh Durham Airport to see them all waiting for me. When we got home, Gena told me she was pregnant with her second child. I was going to be an uncle again, which had new meaning since I'd delivered that little boy in Bethlehem. I thought about Caitlin, and the children I had penciled in to the life we were going to lead together, the life I hadn't focused on enough to give a fighting chance.

I was beyond happy for Gena and Chris. But for some reason all I could think about was going to sleep. I'd never felt so exhausted in my life. I wanted to stay up with my family and celebrate, but I just couldn't.

The next day, after twelve hours of sleep and several cups of coffee, I still wasn't back on track. I had to skip going to the gym with Chris, which I had never done before. That day of rest didn't cure my bone-tiredness. It was as though I had a permanent hangover. After several days of fatigue, I knew something was wrong, but when I discovered enlarged lymph nodes in my groin in the shower a few days later, I began to think it might be serious. I didn't want to alarm my family, so I kept my discovery to myself, but I knew right away that the enlarged lymph nodes might be a sign of cancer. This wasn't the first time my sisters or I had hidden something painful from one another. We'd learned from the best. My mom was a master at shouldering burdens without a word. When she battled cancer, we'd learn about symptoms she was struggling with only when the doctor asked specifically about whether she was experiencing them. She didn't want to burden us, but she also didn't want to lie to the doctor. And, following her lead, my sisters were protectively selective in sharing the specifics of my mom's deteriorating condition with me while I was away at school.

I thought about asking one of the surgeons I had trained under to check me out when I returned to Philadelphia; I thought a lymph node biopsy would make sense. But then I convinced myself I was just suffering from medical student syndrome— a form of hypochondria not uncommon to doctors in training as they learn about the approximately ten thousand diseases currently known to man. I tried to put my health concerns aside and enjoy this precious time with my growing family.

I'm an empiricist. I trust my eyes.

That's not exactly a bold statement coming from a doctor and researcher. Western medicine in the twenty-first century is all about evidence. It's sort of a package deal: the white coat, the stethoscope, and the scientific method. When you're in the healing business, what you really do is test, test some more, test some more, test some more, and—if you're lucky—test a little bit more. You're a professional results gatherer. Every once in a while, one of those results comes back hot: an effective treatment. A new drug. A new procedure.

More often than not, you end up with a dud.

But that's the trade-off, and it's worth it. We trust the process. We trust the evidence.

Which is why moments of intuition are so challenging for some doctors to understand. My own struggle with trusting my intuition is a classic case.

After my vacation in Raleigh, I returned to that same hospital in Bethlehem where I transitioned to my final rotation on outpatient gynecology. But the real transition, the one that was overwhelming me, was of my sluggishness and fatigue turning into something undeniably worse. To keep up, I increased my intake of caffeine pills and energy drinks. I snuck into empty rooms multiple times a day and set my phone alarm for seven minutes later so I could sleep for six. I continued to focus on anything I could except for what had gone wrong with Caitlin and my health.

It was obvious that I was sick. But I didn't just feel sick. Somehow, well before the worst of the symptoms manifested, well before I was incapacitated with organ failure, and well before I was admitted to a hospital and my family gathered . . . I *knew* I was dying. I just *knew*.

That's not exactly accurate. I had a different term for it in my mind: I felt doomed. That "knowledge" arrived well ahead of any evidence.

So much for empiricism. It was a feeling.

That's the only way I know how to describe it. It's like how dogs curl up beside their owners before they die or act erratic before natural disasters. They can sense that something bad is going to happen.

I actually told three of my closest friends, Ben, Grant, and Ron, that I was dying. This was even before I felt sick in all the ways I eventually would. I was just really tired and had a few enlarged lymph nodes—and a sense that things were going to get very bad very quickly. They didn't know how to react. I think they thought I was joking. I wish I was. Perhaps Grant knew something was truly wrong when I was too fatigued to work out. He and I had made a habit of doing pull-ups early each morning on a tree branch outside the dorm in Bethlehem where we were staying for our rotation. Looking back, I can see now that those pull-ups were to be among the final chances I had to build the physical strength I would soon so desperately need. I think Grant welcomed the respite from these early morning tree workouts, but he knew it just wasn't like me not to have the energy or will to do them.

I also became fatalistic. When a new computer that I had just purchased arrived, I returned it and bought a computer with a larger monitor despite the fact that it cost a lot more. I rationalized the expense to myself and my friends by explaining that I deserved the larger screen and didn't need to save money—since I wasn't going to live much longer. Again, my friends didn't know what to say. I wasn't even a garden-variety hypochondriac; they found this strangely dramatic new side of me unnerving.

But the honeymoon phase with death—feeling vaguely bad, flirting with fatalistic proclamations about it, and splurging on larger monitors—was short. Soon, sharp abdominal pain and nausea began to overtake me. The nausea made me skip meals. The abdominal pain would force me to lie in the fetal position or bend over to almost 90 degrees whenever I had to stand. I wouldn't allow myself to do either of those things when I was around patients, so my work interactions became miserable and terrifying. The pain also radiated to my spine, so I asked Grant to try to crack my back during a break between patient visits, hoping that the pain could be relieved with such a simple maneuver. It didn't help—it wasn't my back.

Four days before my end-of-rotation exam, I woke up to find my sheets were drenched in sweat. I stumbled to the sink to get some water and was startled when I detected lumps on both sides of my neck. As I looked at myself in the mirror, it was obvious that I was feeling enlarged lymph nodes, just like those on a young man with lymphoma I had recently cared for. My mind went no further than that. If my hands had been feeling the same lumps on anyone else, I'd already be deep into one of a few diagnostic branching paths: infection? mono? lupus? cancer? But not now, not for myself. I resisted becoming my own patient as long as I could.

The next morning, I noticed that some tiny red bumps on my arms and chest had gotten larger since just a few days before. They looked like balls of blood vessels on my skin. I remember having seen something similar once before, back in my dermatology rotation. They were called blood moles, or cherry hemangiomas, or senile hemangiomas. It's totally normal for them to appear on the skin as we age—hence the name *senile*—but I had never heard of them appearing suddenly like this and growing so rapidly, and on an otherwise healthy(ish) young man.

The pileup of symptoms had become impossible to ignore. But I just needed to make it through the end of my rotation and the exam, only a few more days, and then—I told myself—I could get checked out. I comforted myself with the idea that it was probably just a gallbladder infection causing the stabbing abdominal pain, nausea, and flu-like symptoms. Of course, a gallbladder infection wouldn't explain the blood moles, so, like everyone else in the world, I turned to Google. And, predictably, the results were not comforting. I was directed to a couple of papers from the 1970s and '80s suggesting that the eruption of blood moles could be a sign of cancer. I immediately closed the browser on my big, brand-new computer.

A day before the exam, I slammed two energy drinks as I struggled to make it through morning clinic. My body tem-

perature was swinging between fevers and chills. A thermome-
ter in one of the patient rooms detected a fever of 101.5, and
then my temperature was 95 degrees just a few minutes later.
My resident could see that I didn't look well (although anyone
could have picked up on that), so she told me to go home and
get some rest, and I dutifully left the clinic—and went to the
library to study. I still had my eyes on the prize; and I was still
completely deluded. I didn't make it past the first page of my
notes before I curled up on the floor. The carpet felt like it was
only a millimeter thick above rock-hard cement. I didn't care.
Four hours later, I woke up and it was already time to drive back
to Philadelphia so that Grant and I could take the exam the next
morning. To the great benefit of all the drivers on I-476 that
night, Grant drove.

I think I had some minor fantasy that test day would come
and my body would give me a break for a few hours, but that
remained a fantasy. The fact that I was even able to show up that
day is a credit to my inveterate test taking (I was always the kid
with the multiple, precisely sharpened number 2 pencils on test
day, paging through my notes for the hundredth and final time),
but when I got there this time, it was too much even for me. My
fever was spiking, and the pain in my abdomen was piercing.
My body was drenched from head to toe in sweat. And above
all—I was so, so tired. Beyond tired. I had almost nothing left.

Not ideal conditions for an exam. I struggled to comprehend
the questions on the page in front of me. My mind bobbed up
and down on waves of pain. I couldn't focus. For what seemed
like an eternity, I realized that I had been weighing the virtues
of answering A versus C—but I had no memory of what the
actual question was.

Then I was hit again with that crystal-clear knowledge of my
fate. It didn't matter if I marked A or C, because, I realized, I
was about to die.

After the exam, I stumbled down the hall of that very hospital to the emergency room. A quick look at me told the triage nurse that I needed help. I was hurried into a battery of tests. An ultrasound revealed that my gallbladder was fine, but my blood tests were abnormal, to put it mildly—my liver function, kidney function, and blood counts were, I was told, "all off." The ER doctor felt the enlarged lymph nodes in my neck and announced he was ordering a chest, abdomen, and pelvis CT scan and admitting me for further evaluation.

Suddenly I was wearing a hospital gown, getting wheeled past medical students, residents, and nurses on the same floor of the same hospital I'd worked on. I'd been with a patient who was in the same bed I found myself in, and I'd stood where my doctor now stood, and I was feeling the same fear and uncertainty that I assume my patient had felt. If nothing else, I was getting an education in what a patient really needs in terms of a doctor's bedside manner. But I wasn't looking for silver linings or life lessons that day.

In between the scan and getting the results, I realized I wanted to call my family, but I also wanted to wait until I had more information to share. I hated the idea of making anyone join me in that halfway space of knowing something was wrong but not knowing what that something was. I knew they'd be so worried about me, so I decided to hold off.

The next morning, the attending physician informed me that the CT scan showed enlarged lymph nodes throughout my body and that my blood tests had gotten worse from the day before. He suspected I had lymphoma or another blood-related cancer, but wanted to perform additional tests to see if a virus, though highly unlikely, could be responsible for my symptoms. The doctor was prompt and professional, but I knew what he was saying. All signs were pointing toward aggressive lymphoma. He knew it, and I did too.

This was not the "more information" I was hoping to receive and share with my family.

The cases of lymphoma on my medical school exams almost always began with something like "a previously healthy twenty-five-year-old male presenting with flu-like symptoms, enlarged lymph nodes, and abnormal blood counts." That was me, and the doctors told me as much, but they still weren't certain. After they left my room, I walked out into the hallway. Wearing a hospital gown instead of my usual short white coat, I logged on to one of the computers mounted on the wall and pulled up my CT scan. I reviewed the images over and over, between bouts of pain that folded me in half. Each scan showed the same thing. My body was riddled with enlarged lymph nodes. Fluid had accumulated around my heart, in my lungs, and in my abdomen. With symptoms this pronounced, and developing this quickly, I knew that I had only a few weeks left to live, whether it was lymphoma or not.

Just two weeks ago, my totally nonscientific but deep-seated feeling that I was dying had moved me to upgrade my computer. This time death wasn't a feeling; it was a revelation, and a photographic fact. Its traces were gathering inside my body already, and I could see them faithfully represented in black and white in front of me. I immediately thought of Caitlin. I wanted to call her. But I couldn't. It was six months past our breakup. She had reached out to me once since then, but I'd pushed her away, still hurt and still foolishly thinking that we had all the time in the world for our relationship to work out if and when it was meant to be. I'd been waiting for that timing to become more obvious. My unexpected illness forced me to slow down for the first time since our breakup and recognize the feelings I still had for her.

Then I started to count. In the days and weeks I had left— was there time to get back together? Was there time to be in love again? And, an especially manic thought that I can now see speaks to my underlying desire to simply *have a future:* Was there time to have a child together?

Tears streamed down my face.

The next person I thought of was my best friend, Ben. Ben had been my best friend—more like a brother really—from the first day of high school. A constant supportive presence, Ben continued to be there for me, deep into challenges that surpassed route running and Latin homework. He was one of the friends I had called a couple weeks before to tell about the computer. Now I tried to compose myself before calling him again. But as soon as I started to speak, I burst into tears. "Remember I told you that I thought I was sick, but didn't know what was going on? The doctors think it's lymphoma, and the scans look bad." I struggled to catch my breath. "I don't think I have much time left."

My limited composure quickly decomposed. Between sobs, I told him how sorry I was that I wouldn't be around to be the best man at his hypothetical wedding or to be his future children's godfather, two things that we had promised to each other years before. Ben simply responded that he'd get in his car and be there as soon as he could. And he did, driving seven hours through the night.

Then I called my sisters and dad. Sadly, they knew all too well what to do. They had received this kind of news before. They stopped everything—my dad canceled all surgeries and clinics, my sisters closed up shop—and they flew in the next day. After those calls I was done. I left Caitlin alone. I put away thoughts of reunions and our future.

My blood tests and symptoms continued to worsen, but my outlook only got more confused. The following day, a new set of doctors told me that they didn't think it was lymphoma after all, but that they still didn't know what it was. My family was with me, and we were relieved by the new report, but now I was back to living in that gray zone of uncertainty. I hated being the patient. I wanted to be at the controls. I wanted to find out what was wrong and fix it, *immediately*.

The doctors ordered a battery of additional tests and decided to discharge me forty-eight hours after I'd stumbled into the ER fresh from my exam. They instructed my family to keep a close eye on me and bring me back to the hospital should anything worsen. Back at my apartment, I slept for almost twenty-four hours, with only brief periods of waking, when I guzzled Gatorade to try to quench my insatiable thirst. But I never peed. My father and sisters stayed on couches in my apartment along with Ben, Ron, and Grant to monitor me. We were all scared.

The next morning my legs and belly were swollen with fluid. The water retention was a symptom I'd seen before in patients who were suffering from dysfunction of the liver, kidneys, or heart, but I had never seen it come on so quickly. As I struggled to get out of bed, crushing chest pain hit me like I'd been shot, and I called for my dad. He rushed me back to the ER. An EKG revealed what we already knew: serious cardiac abnormalities. Doctors and nurses rushed in and out of my room, administering several medications and running a series of new tests. Pinned in the middle of a whirlwind of activity, I experienced a strange moment of peace. Like the strange, slow quiet between the first shivering of a Jenga tower and its crashing fall. I wasn't going anywhere anytime soon. Then suddenly came the most intense pain yet, boring into my chest, and a bright flash filled my field of vision. And I was out.

I woke up almost twenty-four hours later in the intensive care unit. I couldn't see anything out of my left eye. I squinted and labored to bring my hands to my face to rub my eyes, but still nothing from my left eye. A retinal hemorrhage, they told me later. Ophthalmologists came, and treatments began.

But my sight was the least of my worries.

Nearly every other part of my body—each of them more critical to my survival than my eyes—was beginning to collapse. First my liver, then my kidneys, then my bone marrow, and then my heart. Laconically called MSOF on the other side of the

patient-doctor divide, I knew this was short for "multiple system organ failure." I'd written it down many times on patient
charts without a lick of understanding about what it actually felt
like.

More tests greeted me when I woke up. Repeated blood
tests, tests for inflammation and immune activation all came
back abnormal. No one knew what was causing this. Soon, I
lost the ability to sit up or stand and struggled to move beyond
just straightening or bending my arm for a blood draw or new
IV. Consciousness came and went. During the fleeting moments
that I was awake, I struggled to think critically and to speak. My
words were slow to form, and they seemed to get completely
lost on the way from my brain to my mouth. There were two
things that I ruminated about during these periods of consciousness. I wondered what I had done to deserve this kind of punishment. *Had I done something or failed to do something that demanded
my endless suffering in return? Had I prayed too little? Had I questioned too much?* I was also fixated on the blood moles on my
body, asking anyone who walked into the room about them.
Doctors, nurses, food deliverers, trash collectors. I just couldn't
stop obsessing about them.

A hematology fellow was visiting me, and I seized the opportunity to bug him. With my eyes closed, I struggled to sum-
mon the strength to lift my hand up to point to a blood mole on
my neck. "What . . . do . . . they . . . mean?" This was a question that I'd apparently already asked several times before. Clearly
frustrated, the hematology fellow pleaded with me, "David,
your liver, your kidneys, your heart, your lungs, and your bone
marrow aren't working properly, and we're trying our best to
figure those really important things out. Please, forget about the
blood moles."

I didn't. Perhaps fixating on them could keep me from thinking about what I was pretty sure was imminent death. Or maybe

they gave me something simple enough that I could focus on and feel like I was assisting in my care. My own health was giving me a technical reprieve from medicine, but figuring out what these blood moles meant would help me get back in the proverbial saddle.

But not yet.

Within two weeks, I'd radically transformed. I came into the hospital weighing 215 pounds and in obsessively athletic shape. Then, I gained 90 pounds of fluid weight, and I lost 50 pounds of muscle. My failing liver wasn't producing a key factor to prevent fluid from leaking out of my blood vessels, so fluid rushed into my abdomen, legs, arms, and the sacs around my heart, lungs, and liver. My doctors administered liters of IV fluids to try to maintain enough blood in my vessels for my heart to pump to my vital organs, but it continued to leak out, as a substance called extracellular fluid—basically everything in blood except the blood cells themselves. Water and protein, mostly. The fluid caused the sacs around my organs to stretch beyond capacity. I caught myself screaming often. I was given high doses of opioid painkillers, but they didn't help. The opioids only made my thinking blurrier and caused me to hallucinate— I saw teddy bear–looking creatures walking on the walls of my room—a bizarre nightmare when you are simultaneously experiencing knifing pains throughout your body.

Trauma surgeons debated opening up my abdomen to search for a cause for my symptoms and a source of the abdominal pain, but my blood counts were too low to safely operate. Fortunately, breaking bones on the football field had heightened my pain threshold and helped me to breathe through some of the pain. And the muscle mass I had gained over years of high-intensity training served as a vital protein source, which helped to keep me alive while my immune system was ravaging so much of my body. There was a flurry of activity after my father rushed back with me to the ER and after I passed out for twenty-four hours, but there was little to show for it. As my disease ran rampant, countless tests—bone marrow biopsies, PET scans, MRIs, a renal arteriogram, a transjugular liver biopsy—failed to identify what exactly was killing me.

CHAPTER SIX

I LAY MOTIONLESS in bed for weeks.

It was often dark.

Medication helped the sight to return in my left eye, but bright lights were difficult for my fragile vision to endure, so we kept the lights off in my room. Nausea was my constant companion. I threw up every small bite I tried to eat over those first few weeks. I continued to drift in and out of consciousness. Even my brain was under attack, and between lucid moments I could feel it grinding to a halt. In the limbo between conscious and unconscious states, it could take me minutes to respond even to simple yes-or-no questions.

I understood that whatever I was suffering from was mysterious, but I also began to notice that there were other reasons my diagnosis was proving elusive. I got glimpses of the situation when my doctors were in my room and I was partially alert. The nephrologists and rheumatologists thought it was lymphoma. Oncologists thought it was an infectious disease. Infectious disease specialists thought the issue was rheumatologic. The critical care team didn't know what it was.

As my medical school friends scoured through textbooks and medical journals to try to find answers, the refrain of my doctors became "No one knows."

Meanwhile, my family knew exactly what I needed. My dad and my sisters (Gena was now three months pregnant) stayed by my side even when that meant defying instructions to keep out of my room in case some dangerous, exotic virus was the source of my ailments. I believe that their encouragement and presence saved my life. This inexplicable attack caught me flat-footed and unprepared, and in those first days and weeks, at times, I was ready to give up. Those words—*give up*—don't quite translate across the barrier between the ailing and the well, and, even now, I've lost some touch with what it once meant in the moment, mentally, to give in to death. But I remember doing so. Death seemed to promise me peace and an end to my suffering, and that was alluring at a time when every breath was painful. The harder I pushed to breathe sufficiently deeply, the more knifelike pain I felt. So I slowed my breathing and fought less for each breath. I thought about my patient George and how he was ready to give up before he reconnected with his daughter. Likewise, it was my family, with whatever special sensitivity only families can have, who must have realized I was slipping away, and it was their urging that brought me back. "Just breathe," I remember hearing. That was enough. I snapped out of my trance and began fighting for each breath again.

They also put in work outside of my room. Gena tracked down labs and talked to doctors about the possible diagnoses. She spent hours at night with Ron and Grant discussing results from tests that were run, what the diagnosis could be, and what additional tests should be run. I was glad someone else was gathering as much data as possible. I also think all the activity helped her to cope.

Lisa focused her energy on how I was feeling and what she could do to help keep AMF afloat. She distanced herself from what the testing meant or what could happen to me so that she wasn't too emotionally overwhelmed to be there for me. I understood that approach too. Cognitive overload is real, especially in a hyperactive environment like a hospital.

My dad, true to form, took his own approach. I knew he was in pain himself. In some ways he was in his element—he was an orthopedic surgeon familiar with patients in dire need of fixing—but he struggled in this helpless situation just as he had struggled when he was unable to help my mom. Here was a patient he couldn't fix. There was no rolling up his sleeves and getting to work. There wasn't anything to *do*, because no one knew what disease needed to be stopped. He was powerless. But he didn't check out. He looked at lab results he hadn't seen since medical school and slept in the hospital room on a fold-out chair every single night so that I was never alone. He even pleaded with ICU doctors to take care of his baby boy. And sometimes, I now know, he just shut down and cried. But my family never cried in my room, just in the halls. They remembered what I had said to them seven years before about not crying in my mom's room after her brain surgery, and they took the same tack with me. But my shift in perspective from caregiver to patient taught me something very important: It was okay for my loved ones to cry. It didn't add to my stresses; it showed me they cared.

My sisters and I had grown closer after my mom's death, but my dad and I had grown apart. I had focused every day on how to keep her spirit alive through AMF and my medical training, while he understandably struggled to talk about her or relive memories. Our different strategies for carrying on disconnected us, though it was never a difference over substance, just method. Despite the distance that had grown between us, there was now not a hint of difficulty during my illness. In fact we grew closer than ever.

Eventually he found a way to put his medical background directly to use. Unbeknownst to me, a family friend gave my dad the cellphone number of someone at the National Institutes of Health. My dad didn't know who this doctor was or what he did, but that didn't deter him and he wasn't interested in asking. This wasn't a social call. He had heard this doctor would be helpful, and he wanted answers about his son. My dad called at least once a day, often keeping this busy doctor on the phone for thirty to forty-five minutes at a time, and he would shout into the phone about the latest developments: "Hey, Foochi, I've got more results I want your thoughts on." Then he would rattle off results and questions. I later asked my dad who this "Dr. Foochi" was that he had called so much, and he didn't know, so I availed myself of Google . . . and was mortified. It was Dr. Tony Fauci (pronounced "Fowchi")—*the* Dr. Tony Fauci—director of the National Institute of Allergy and Infectious Diseases, and one of the most revered physician-scientists in the world. Fauci was a presidential adviser, he'd helped develop George W. Bush's President's Emergency Plan for AIDS Relief—he'd won a *Presidential Medal of Freedom*. My dad had never been one for credentials and certainly didn't care about them now. He would have done anything to get answers for his son, even hound a director at the NIH.

Everyone was put into difficult positions. Following the retinal hemorrhage, I'd been given IV blood thinners to try to restore my vision and prevent something similar from happening again. But then one of my IV lines became dislodged and my blood was spilling onto the floor as if from an open faucet because of the blood thinners. Lisa was there and ran to get a nurse, who initiated a cascade of events—such as replacing the IV and reducing my dosage of blood thinners—that stabilized me. This was an important moment for Lisa, who'd always fainted at the sight of blood and needles and had been walking out of the room every time I had a procedure or a blood draw because she thought that she'd pass out. Since she didn't faint this time, she was emboldened and thrilled to stay by my side in the room for a procedure later that night. But she'd clearly gotten ahead of herself, because she fainted and fell to the floor instead, resulting in an "adult rapid response team" to attend to her. Gena, meanwhile, was not happy that any of the medical professionals were focusing any of their attention away from her baby brother. Lisa woke up to a team of doctors and nurses checking on her and Gena shooting her a look.

Throughout these first few weeks in the hospital, Ben was there for me too, and I was able to confide in him during moments of consciousness about some hopes and fears I had that I felt I couldn't share with my sisters or father. More than anything, we talked about Caitlin. We talked about whether someone should contact her and whether it would be a good idea for her to visit. I didn't want her to remember me in the state that I was in. I'd been so uncommunicative, unable to really speak when she broke up with me. Now, of course, there was so much that I wanted to talk to her about, but I knew I didn't have the strength or mental acuity to have the kind of conversation that I wanted to have. I wanted to talk to her about the feelings I still had for her and the future. I felt naïve admitting that to myself, but it was true. It was hard to think of what to say about the future when I still had no idea what kind of future I had, if I had one at all.

As I got sicker, I could no longer think clearly about Caitlin or discuss my health. My conversations with Ben turned to what I'd do if I survived—and what I'd need to do if I wasn't going to survive. We agreed on small things that nevertheless felt momentous, and it lifted my spirits just thinking about them. If I made it, we agreed we'd go on a road trip to the Grand Canyon, and we promised that'd be the start of an annual road-trip trend.

If I wasn't going to make it, we discussed how I'd need to say goodbye to my family and friends before it was too late. Apparently, we discussed this many times. Since then, Ben has told me we kept having the same painful conversation over and over because my mind and memory were getting so slippery.

And then, on day twenty in the hospital, we put that plan into practice. I was approaching the nadir of my illness and the likely point of no return. My brain fumbled through thoughts and was turned off most of the day; my lungs, abdomen, and legs were filled with fluid; and I hadn't walked in almost three weeks. My doctors were running out of tests to do, but still didn't have a diagnosis. Ben contacted my closest friends so they could come visit one last time.

And they came. Nine friends and my uncle Michael visited over the course of three days. It was like office hours of the dying man: Each friend came in alone and stayed about half an hour. There were a lot of tears. The early visitors were luckier: With every day and every new visitor, I became less able to hold a conversation. Each goodbye was final.

I know that they all would have given anything to help me get better. I faintly remember Liam, my six-foot-seven friend and former offensive lineman at Georgetown, offering a lung, a kidney, or a portion of his liver to me. My dad had just walked into the room and replied that he didn't think the organs could help me because I couldn't survive a transplant procedure. Then, he joked that Liam's organs likely wouldn't fit in me anyway.

One friend's visit provided what was possibly the last moment of pure, unadulterated joy I could count on. Francisco was a medical student too, which meant that when he leaned in to hug me in my bed—exercising superb bedside manner, I would add—his stethoscope slammed into my forehead. No problem—*if* you have a normal number of blood platelets coursing through your body, preventing bleeding problems. You probably have between 150,000 and 450,000 right now. I had fewer than 10,000, which put me at constant risk for a deadly brain bleed that could be triggered with the slightest trauma.

Francisco and I looked at each other, both frozen, wordlessly wondering if his hug had just triggered a bleed that would kill me right then and there. When we realized I was in the clear, we laughed. Humor was never as distant as I would have guessed. Death seemed sometimes to have a kind of gravitational pull that inverted its own darkness. After everything I was going through, my friend almost poked me to death. It *was* funny.

The risks of bruising and trauma aside, a physical therapist came into my room shortly thereafter to ask if he could help me walk. One of my nurses had sternly warned me the day before that if I didn't muster up the strength to stand and overcome the pain of movement, I would never get out of the hospital. I wasn't sure I was going to ever get out of the hospital anyway, but I was desperate to give it a try.

Just sitting up in bed made me short of breath. It had been almost a month since I had walked—or stood, for that matter. But with Francisco by my side—he had been my weight-lifting partner, and the sturdiest spotter I'd ever known—I walked from my room to the nurses' station, about twenty-five feet away, and back. At first, my legs didn't move the way I was trying to instruct them to. It was as if I had forgotten how to walk. Muscle memory soon kicked in, but then it was my heart and lungs' turn to struggle to keep up with my activity. I was completely out of breath by the fifth step. I had to take a break from my walk for some apple juice before returning to the ICU bed. Once I was back in, Francisco and I said a painful goodbye.

Three years later, Francisco was paralyzed in a motorcycle accident and lost his ability to walk. He was an emergency medicine resident at Harvard at the time. Amazingly, he returned to his residency program and later became the first person in a wheelchair to graduate from an emergency medicine residency; he inspires me every day.

When my friend Grant came to say goodbye, he wasn't able to keep up the façade that everyone else had. He's since described to me the horror of my appearance that day. My formerly muscular legs were bloated barrels with little form. Fluid had expanded all parts of my body, yet my face was thin and sunken, covered in weeks of scruff since shaving was too dangerous with my low platelet count. The expression on his face told me how terrible I looked at that point, how much my body had transformed. I hadn't looked in a mirror in weeks, but now I didn't need to.

And then one more person came. She came without my asking. In fact, she came despite my hopes that she wouldn't learn of my condition. But I couldn't stop the inevitable spread of information, especially when it flowed through channels of good intentions and modern convenience. It was Caitlin's mother, Patty, who'd gotten an email a couple days earlier with a link to a CaringBridge page and another email requesting that she pray for one David Fajgenbaum. Patty, hoping it was another David Fajgenbaum (though there aren't too many of us), called my cell. My dad answered and explained what was going on. He didn't beat around the bush: I was getting worse every day and no one knew what the diagnosis was.

I woke up momentarily on the afternoon after Francisco's visit, and my father was there. He told me about Patty, about the email, about her call.

He told me she was coming to see me. With Caitlin, who had graduated from college and was working in the fashion industry in New York.

I'd thought about Caitlin every day since I first went to the ER. I'd thought about what this would be like, to see her one more time. I'd discussed with Ben whether it was right, or best, for me or for her. And I'd made a decision. It came down to this: I didn't want this to be her last memory of me. I was immobilized in bed, I was sick, and I was weak, both physically and mentally. I struggled to communicate, period, and could barely piece together complete or complex thoughts.

My wish to die without Caitlin seeing me in this state was undoubtedly linked to my experience with my mom: The vision of her weakened by cancer just before she passed away was burned into my memory. I pictured Caitlin remembering me in my debilitated state years and even decades after I was gone—just as I now remembered my mom. That wasn't the picture of my mother that she or I wanted me to hold on to. I wasn't myself, and I didn't want Caitlin to remember me like this.

So, I held my ground. I told my sisters that I didn't want her to see me. When Caitlin and Patty arrived the next morning, my sisters stopped them in the hospital lobby. I can't imagine how awful this must have been for everyone. Caitlin and Patty were devastated, confused, and sad. They said they didn't care how I looked. They just wanted to see me. They reluctantly walked out, hoping that my sisters would come back down to get them. My sisters never did. I asked them not to. I regret that now.

After Caitlin came, and after I denied her access, and after I had said my goodbyes to my family and friends, I settled in to die. Nothing, ever, was worse than that. My health would actually deteriorate further—I would get closer to death still. But it was never like that, never again. I would never again give myself over to inevitability. My memories from those hours and days are tiled together into a kind of kaleidoscope vision. My consciousness was strained to breaking, but I remember reflecting on my life, thinking about my legacy and my obituary. I stared endlessly out of my hospital window, dreaming of what could have been with Caitlin and my life, but knowing I would never step outside again. I remember regretting nothing I'd ever done, only those things I hadn't done or hadn't said. And I remember praying.

CHAPTER SEVEN

AFTER FOUR WEEKS in the hospital, my family decided to airlift me to the hospital my dad had worked at in Raleigh. I assumed they were moving me closer to home for the funeral service. But their intention was to try to take back some control of the situation—by moving me to a hospital where they knew the doctors, the nurses, and the building.

I still didn't have a diagnosis.

In Raleigh, I made my home in the ICU at Rex Hospital, less than a mile down the road from Carter-Finley Stadium, where the heroes of my youth on the NC State Wolfpack football team and thousands of screaming fans had inspired my obsession with playing college football. I had prayed for miracles in that stadium many times as a kid, which never seemed to come true, and I had cried after losses.

Though the stakes were different, I could relate with my younger self. There were more tests. There was more activity. There was even less to show for it.

I remember my eyes focusing on something next to my

bed—and realizing after some time that I was looking at a telephone cord. My sisters had just left the room, so I understood I was alone. By this point, my thought processes had been mostly rubbed away and I had been reduced to thinking in simple, combinatorial ways: I was alone, I was suffering, my death was imminent, my family was suffering as they watched me, and there was an object that could do something about all this. The idea brought me anguish but also relief. I didn't want to die, but it made sense that I should speed up what was inevitable. There is a universe in which my next thoughts coincided with moving my arms over to the cord, wrapping it around my neck, closing my eyes, and never waking again. Finally, relief from a living hell. But fortunately that's not this universe. Instead, and perhaps this signaled the first moments of rehabilitation, my thoughts went to my family and how killing myself would actually add to their trauma. That's where my thoughts stayed, and then stopped.

Then, for no discernible reason, I stabilized. I began to get better. My liver and kidney function tests improved, the fluid around my lungs and heart began to subside, which lessened the pain. The blood moles began to shrink. My red blood cell and platelet transfusions became less frequent. My nausea and vomiting subsided, so I could eat my first meal in five weeks. I walked half a lap around the ICU. Then, I walked a whole lap around the ICU. Early on in my hospitalization at Penn, doctors had begun pumping me full of high-dose corticosteroids—something you do in the ICU when you don't know what else to do. Though there had been no immediate change in my condition, perhaps the cumulative weeks of this treatment had something to do with my improvement. My mind started to come back online too. The telephone cord next to my bed was just a ratty old hospital telephone cord. A nuisance and an anachronism. Nothing more.

I laughed for the first time in a while too, perhaps since

Francisco had poked me. After one of my walks, an ICU doctor came into my room. We knew him well, by that point. Among me and my sisters, he was an established character: He kept coming in and trying to impress us with how he'd gone to this college and that medical school and had that degree. It was tiresome, but not exactly rare in medicine. We just rolled our eyes. This time, though, he drew his material from another source. He looked at me sternly and said, "Before you go on more walks, we need to get you—um, what's the word?" He paused.

"I was in Italy for the last week, so my brain is still thinking in Italian and I can't think of the word in English . . . ah . . . rubber . . . sole . . ." This time, his pause lasted for even longer.

"Oh! *Sandals*. We need to get you sandals so you don't get any blisters since you haven't walked in so long."

He grinned at my sister Gena. It was incredible. He was trying to simultaneously impress a decrepit ICU patient, flirt a little with that patient's pregnant sister, and humbly brag about his jet-set lifestyle. He left, and we cracked up. It felt amazing to be laughing again and, I have to admit, just as amazing to bond over someone else's ridiculousness.

I was finally discharged after seven weeks of hospitalization, mostly in the ICU. I was better—and yet I was no closer to knowing what was wrong with me than on day one.

On the way out, I asked another ICU doctor what he thought had almost killed me (I knew it had become a topic of conversation—doctors love a good mystery), and he said, "I don't know what it was, but let's hope it doesn't come back." His passive use of the word *hope* rattled me.

Soon I learned about thousands of people who had been praying for me, daily. I heard about nuns in Trinidad (where nearly all of my extended family still lives) praying for my health. Friends and family and supporters—a category of people I knew all too well from my life leading AMF—told me about how much they had prayed for my recovery, and how happy they were that I was better.

I was appreciative of the prayers, but a little skeptical of some of the commentary. Some friends and family assured me it was the prayers that saved my life and that the illness wasn't going to come back because it was a test from God, which I had passed. Apparently, God was keeping track of how many people prayed for me before making a judgment, and He didn't test twice. I understood what they were trying to say, but I recalled feeling the same way about my mom after the first postsurgical MRI didn't show any sign of cancer. *Now she was free; she beat it.* We continued to pray. And then I recalled when it *did* come back and our prayers couldn't save her. Others told me that God had saved me because there was still more for me to accomplish in this world. But I knew that I was no more deserving or capable than my mom or any of my patients who hadn't made it. I tried to put these thoughts out of my mind.

I was thrilled to have something else to think about: Caitlin. Being incapacitated for weeks had finally given me time to reflect on how much I cared about and missed her. Shortly after I returned home from my lengthy hospitalization, I got up the courage to call her and tried to explain why I had insisted she not see me in my near-death state. This was a very difficult conversation—my keeping her from seeing me had hurt her deeply. She told me that it was okay; she accepted my explanation that I just didn't want her to see me—and remember me—in such a weak state. Since then, I've learned that she didn't actually buy my explanation—she thought it was my sisters who didn't think she should see me and that I was just covering for them.

Talking to Caitlin again made me feel something even better than healthy: It made me feel normal. It was awkward sometimes, but it was mostly like old times, it was great. We avoided talking about getting back together, though she did invite me to come up to New York for Halloween. We left it at that—I didn't know if my health would allow it just yet. But it felt great to be asked.

Soon thereafter, Caitlin's parents traveled to Raleigh for a previously planned trip. They stopped by my dad's house, and we took a walk together. I was thrilled to have them visit. Patty was more like my mom than anyone I had ever met, infinitely proud of her children, strong in her principles, and always ready to help anyone in need (our immediate connection helped us to quickly get past the shirt-ripping episode from that high school basketball game years before). Caitlin's dad, Bernie, was both an amazing father and a big-time TV executive. He also managed to devote meaningful time as a board member of several local charities. I admired his ability to live seemingly multiple lives at once—and in balance.

They didn't let on even the slightest bit of frustration that I hadn't let Patty and Caitlin see me when I was so sick. I think they were just so glad to see me looking so well. Patty asked if I was going to slow down a bit in my relentless pursuit of growing AMF and training to become a physician after my near-death experience (which is how we were beginning to speak of it). I started to explain that I thought I would indeed probably slow down and not work such long hours. But Bernie wasn't so sure. He had friends, he explained, who'd had heart attacks and strokes and cancer diagnoses. They all said they'd change, but not one of them really did. He hoped I'd be different. I would soon join their ranks—slowing down wasn't in my future.

That's not to say, however, that I didn't learn another lesson from that first brush with death. Perhaps because I'd had a group of caring people gather around my bedside, I became conscious of whom they had seen before them and why they were there; I saw in sharp focus that I needed to live every day the way I'd want the people I love to remember me when they're crowded around me on my last day. My mother did this. Her demeanor was a living legacy: generous, wise, and warm. Not just on good days, and not as she was presented with her own mortality. Always.

With clarity I now saw that the showdown with Patty and Caitlin in the hospital lobby was a result of my not making Caitlin a priority before we broke up, not fighting for her after we were apart, and feeling terrible that I'd not done so. With a new lease on life—and for however long it lasted—I decided I didn't want to be remembered as a person "too busy" for things, even if what I'd been busy doing felt important. If I was given the chance, I wanted to be remembered as a great partner, an amazing father, a generous friend, and a disease curer. I vowed I would make time for the people I loved. I would not wait.

Nor would I wait to figure out what I'd just been through. I wasn't at all satisfied with just "becoming better" in a mysterious way after a mysterious illness. I wanted answers.

I began by requesting and reviewing my own medical records dating back to childhood. This wasn't just my morbid curiosity. I knew that a disease that seemingly went away on its own would have no issue with coming back. For all I knew, it was just temporarily dormant. I needed to figure it out before it woke back up. I had been a patient, and I had been a doctor in training, and I liked being the latter a whole lot more.

So, I began my work. I received over three thousand pages of records and reconstructed my own medical history. I started working on my differential diagnosis, or a list of possible diagnoses that *could* be causing my particular set of symptoms or problems. Then, I applied the available data to evaluate each diagnosis in turn to start narrowing down the possibilities. This was an exercise that I had done frequently for other patients on my clinical rotations just months before. Now, and for more than twelve hours a day, I scanned medical records and papers to identify patterns that might have any relevance to what I'd just gone through.

My focus was laser-like, but I did have one very welcome (and frequent) distraction: bathroom breaks. My kidneys and liver, which hadn't worked for two months, finally returned to full function again. I was peeing out all of the fluid that had accumulated in my body. I urinated 42 pounds of fluid in fourteen days as my fluid-filled belly and edema-swollen legs shrank. Suddenly I weighed 165 pounds, 50 less than when I was admitted to the hospital at Penn, and a weight I don't think I'd seen since junior high school. But I'd take it. It was amazing. I was urinating myself back to normal.

And then I started getting tired again.

CHAPTER EIGHT

THE IMMUNE SYSTEM is staggeringly complex.

That means that attempts to describe what it does, and *how* it does what it does, quickly run into one challenge above all: the relative conceptual poverty of any available metaphors. You'll have encountered this challenge if you recall your typical high school–level biology class. Many earnest textbook writers have tried to describe the immune system in lay terms. Is it like an alarm system? Or is it like a power grid, or first responders, or an army? That last one is perhaps the most appropriate, and I've heard it used countless times: Our bodies are fortresses, and our white blood cells include many specialized soldiers and hunter-killers that seek out invading pathogens and cancers. The rest fills itself out. There are lines of communication. There are battles. There are winners and losers.

To be honest, the military imagery may be a bit overdramatic, but it is pretty accurate based on what we know.

Consider: Our immune cells have receptors on their surfaces that can detect whether something is a friend or a foe. That's a basic component of the whole apparatus, and one that we do understand fairly well. Alas, as in any good arms race, many adversary cells have evolved ways to mask their outsiderness, or even mimic the appearance of healthy cells. But when that mimicry fails, when our immune cells successfully detect an enemy, they release molecules called cytokines that trigger an array of initiatives:

1. Alerting other immune cells to what they've detected
2. Notifying specialized killer immune cells that they should go into attack mode
3. Attracting other cells into the appropriate area
4. And, finally, coordinating when to stop the barrage.

If *any* aspect of those immune responses goes wrong—say a false alert is sounded or the specialized killer cells go after the wrong target or the signal to stop isn't received—your healthy cells will almost certainly suffer. It takes only one misstep. But then consider that each of the four simplified steps I just listed is actually made up of thousands of smaller steps and connections, each in itself a complex interplay among thousands of genes and hundreds of molecules that must bind to specific cell receptors and in turn trigger cellular procedures that lead to the production of additional molecules. It's triggers all the way down. And then there are triggers all the way back up to feed back to the triggers that they should continue or stop. And these steps are all occurring simultaneously in billions of cells that represent hundreds of different specialized types of immune cells. To say there is a lot going on is an understatement.

And it happens all day, every day, all over your body.

Just one error in the genetic code or one mistake in an immune response can be deadly, because its effect multiplies as it cascades throughout the system.

Militaries make mistakes all the time. Supplies are lost, equipment degrades, and, in tragic scenarios, armies can even accidentally fire on themselves.

But imagine if friendly fire triggered more friendly fire.

Which triggered more friendly fire.

Which triggered more friendly fire.

And all this assumes that we know everything there is to know about the interactions and functions of the immune system. We don't.

After getting discharged from Rex, I split my time between my dad's house and my sister Gena's. It was easier on them both that way. I was sensitive about putting all of my responsibilities on just one person, even though I'm positive either would have been happy to host and help me full-time.

Three weeks later, I was staying with Gena. I'd been feeling extra-tired all day, but I was happy to chalk it up to continued recovery; it made sense that my body would take a while to bounce back fully from being at death's door. But that night before I went to bed, I noticed that some of the blood moles on my chest and arms that had shrunk away as I recovered were now growing again. Red and livid against my pale skin. Worse than that: New ones had appeared.

My fatigue overwhelmed my mounting anxiety, and I fell asleep. Fourteen hours later, Gena decided it was time to wake me up. I was still exhausted.

Then, with horrible punctuality, the nausea and abdominal pain returned, and the fluid shortly after. I got some dutiful blood work done to confirm what we already knew. This strange and aggressive thing was back.

After four weeks out, I was back in the hospital on November 1, 2010. At Rex, they administered high-dose corticosteroids again, and again there seemed to be no effect from what almost always makes patients feel better and sometimes improves their mysterious ailments.

There was a new twist this time though. My doctor was a

familiar face. In fact, I had once wanted to be him. Just a few months before, he'd met with me when I wanted to discuss my career. I wanted to learn from him. He'd been my mom's on-cologist.

Like the team of doctors before him, he looked at the tests and my symptoms and came to the conclusion that whatever I had wasn't lymphoma. A few months ago, I would have taken his word as the gospel truth, but by this point I'd started to de-velop an ornery streak. Even though my mystery illness had interrupted my medical education, it had somehow given me a kind of candidness I'd lacked when I was healthy and whole. Perhaps it was just the mentality of a man walking the plank: There was nothing to lose now.

So when my mom's oncologist told me I didn't have lym-phoma, I pushed back. I told him about the papers I had found from the 1970s and '80s suggesting that the eruption of these blood moles might indeed be a sign of an underlying malig-nancy, that that malignancy might indeed be lymphoma. My lymph nodes were enlarged, and I had all of the symptoms. But no one had done the definitive test for lymphoma—a lymph node biopsy. I laid out my case for the surgery as though I were an experienced internist. He responded as though I were an intern.

"You need to be the patient. Let me be the doctor," he said, sternly, and a bit harshly, but not incorrectly.

I was being scolded. And I would normally not press the matter further in a situation like this, especially not with this man I had revered. But I stewed. I thought: *I've been the patient for the last eleven weeks, and no one can figure this shit out.* The fact that no one knew anything was hard to take when I first got sick; it was becoming unacceptable now that I was relapsing.

"Well, what is it?" I nearly screamed.

"I don't know, but I'll eat my shoe if it's lymphoma," he said.

My family was frustrated too. We'd all been deferring to

physicians for weeks and had little to show for it except for a consensus that I *didn't* have lymphoma despite the fact that the definitive test hadn't been done. I guess process of elimination had to start somewhere, but you need the test result to actually rule it out. I didn't know how much longer we had to go through the list. My blood work was showing that my liver, kidneys, and bone marrow were beginning to fail again.

The corticosteroids that had likely saved my life last time still weren't working this time around. So, finally, after several more inconclusive tests, my doctor ordered a lymph node biopsy. It was a relief. It's not that I was convinced I had lymphoma; it's just that it was the most likely conclusion based on the differential diagnosis exercise I'd been going through. I was tired of guesses and supposition. I wanted the hard stuff, I wanted to see results. I was tired of trusting doctors' opinions and hoping for them to find answers. As a physician in training and the son of a physician, I knew that we were not infallible or all knowing. Not even close.

The results came back via fax on a Friday morning. My doctor was out of town.

His nurse-practitioner came into my room to deliver the diagnosis, the test results literally in hand. It happened to be one of the first times in almost three months of being hospitalized that I was alone in my room. I have seen good news delivered, and I have seen bad news delivered. I have seen nurses and doctors with good poker faces and with bad. She did not have a good poker face. She was clearly giddy.

"Good news. It's not lymphoma! You have . . ." And here she read from the fax. "You have HHV-8–negative, idiopathic multicentric Castleman disease. I've never heard of it, so I can't answer any questions about it, but it's not lymphoma! Your doctor can tell you more when he returns next week." She smiled and walked out of the room.

My oncologist would not have to eat his shoe. It really, truly wasn't lymphoma. Even better—I wasn't suffering from some mystery illness anymore. It had a name—I vaguely remembered hearing it once before in my immunology course in medical school, and that must mean it had a history, and clinical trials, and treatments . . . I was excited just for the prospect of being able to *know* this thing.

So, like anyone else, I googled it. Right then and there on my iPhone from my hospital bed.

I scrolled down through the Wikipedia page until I could find some hard data. And there it was, the only study cited, from 1996: Patients with multicentric Castleman disease survive for an average of one year after diagnosis and only one in eight survive for more than two years. They die from multiple system organ failure, MSOF. Which meant, in fact, that this was significantly worse than lymphoma—which we'd all been thinking was the worst-case scenario. It was an incredible moment. A psychological perfect storm. I'd rationalized my morbid insistence on a lymph node biopsy with the hedge that if I was wrong about the possibility of lymphoma, I'd at least be wrong *in the right direction*. I thought I'd have been only happy to be wrong. I didn't even consider that there might have been something worse. I'd been outflanked.

Alone in that room, I cried uncontrollably. For a second time, I knew two things suddenly and simultaneously: I was going to die, and I would never have a future with Caitlin.

As it turned out, besides the survival rate, what was known about idiopathic multicentric Castleman disease at that time was that—for an unknown cause—enlarged lymph nodes produce substances that lead to vital organ failure and death. To return to the military analogy, this isn't just friendly fire begetting more friendly fire. It's like the military dropping a nuclear bomb on every major city it was supposed to be defending. I explained it to my sisters and dad after they returned to my room. My grandparents and aunts arrived from Trinidad a few days later. We tried to be positive. At least now we had a name to curse. Mostly, we cried. And we prayed.

For weeks, I had wanted to uncloak my adversary, so that I could size it up, come up with a game plan, and relentlessly fight it. But little was known about this adversary beyond its name, so I would need to find a physician with expertise and the requisite tools to give me a fighting chance.

We soon learned about a physician at Duke with "some experience," so I was moved to the hematology/oncology ward at Duke. The sign AT DUKE, THERE IS HOPE didn't provide the same comfort that it had seven years before, when I saw it hanging in the waiting room while my mom was undergoing brain surgery. Every day, teams of five to eight physicians and doctors in training would come into the room to discuss my case and observe me. My new team agreed that the corticosteroids weren't working and that the next step would be treatment with a chemotherapy agent. They were also candid with us about how little experience they had—the physician we'd heard of with "some experience" had actually treated only "a few" Castleman disease patients and none with my subtype. I felt like an experiment, and my family quickly grew frustrated because nothing seemed to change, even after the chemotherapy was administered. I just got worse. My doctors stayed the course. There wasn't anything else they knew to do.

They did want to make sure I was at least getting nutrition. I had been vomiting any time I tried to eat, so the team decided to place a feeding tube through my nose down into my stomach to pump in liquid nutrition. Every time the tube got blocked— a not infrequent occurrence—they pulled it out and placed a new one. I'm not sure which was worse. Both directions were pretty terrible. I had done this frequently as a medical student without ever realizing the pain or disgusting tastes that accompany it. I had an insight: Maybe all of us doctors should have some of these procedures done on us a couple times during medical school so we can understand what they're like.

At Duke, I got worse, and worse, and worse, and then I fell off a cliff. I went through MSOF again, and again I felt the whole-body pain of simultaneous organ collapse. I lay in my hospital bed, parts of my body filling with fluid, my organs shutting down, my consciousness flickering on and off like an old television set. Once again my memories grew seams and slipped apart from one another. "You can endure anything for a day," I said, to Gena, I think.

I was at the precipice of death. The simultaneous failures of my kidneys and liver were causing toxins to accumulate in my blood in sufficient concentrations to keep me unconscious and to forestall whole days and weeks of memories from ever forming. Sometimes I wish the memory blankness was more comprehensive. Some memories serve little purpose if you go on living. For instance, there's this: I remember when my family summoned the priest. He didn't come for a social visit. He was there to administer last rites at my hospital bed. I don't recall the laying of hands, or the oil; I do remember it was dark and I was scared to die.

And for a second time, Caitlin came to see me, this time flying down to North Carolina. Though I'd recently had the epiphany that I would prioritize the people I loved, I was still not ready for her to see me. One of the only coherent sentences I spoke over a two-week period was to tell my sisters that I didn't want Caitlin to visit. I didn't want her to remember me like this. Lisa texted Caitlin to let her know that now wasn't a good time without letting on that I was getting worse by the day and approaching death's door. Caitlin filled her time in Raleigh by visiting friends as she waited for news about a good time to come to the hospital—totally unaware of just how sick I was or that I could die at any moment—before she flew back to New York. She left heartbroken again. I regret to this day that for a second time I turned her away.

I'd been anointed and blessed and sent on my way to die. Then the chemo kicked in. And the drugs kept me tethered to where I was, at least for the time being. It could not have happened any later. It had taken eleven weeks from my first hospitalization to be diagnosed with idiopathic multicentric Castleman disease and receive my first chemotherapy treatment. If it had taken eleven weeks and one day, I probably wouldn't have survived. I barely did anyway.

I had now experienced twice in three months a rough equivalent of dying. It was likely I would again, but I knew what happened to your odds the longer you played Russian roulette. So I didn't celebrate when I was awake and cognizant again. I could not accept living like that. I couldn't accept living in between almost dying, or what that was doing to my family, or what it was making me do to Caitlin. I was done not knowing. I was done hoping that my doctors would get lucky. I was done making my family prepare to let me die. I was done turning the love of my life away so she wouldn't have to remember me as a confused, bloated ghoul. From that point on, I was going to take control of my life as much as my body would allow me. I would face up to idiopathic multicentric Castleman disease, or iMCD, take it on like an adversary. My tactics would change over time, but the mission remained clear.

For the time being, I put on a happy face as I slowly recovered in the hospital. And I *was* happy. I was grateful to be alive and too focused on my next steps to waste any time—even a moment—on self-pity or sadness. It was late November now, so my dad cooked Thanksgiving dinner and brought it to my bedside. I had had my feeding tube removed, so my sisters, dad, several family friends, and I ate a feast together. It was my first real meal in weeks, and I got to feel normal for an afternoon. After the meal my sisters and I watched *Borat* and *Saturday Night Live* clips on YouTube and laughed and talked about absolutely nothing important.

The next morning, I got to work from my hospital room.

CHAPTER NINE

UPTODATE IS THE top online resource that doctors use to collect and access all the latest knowledge on any number of subjects, including diseases and treatments. It's trustworthy because it's made by doctors and for doctors. And it's kept up to date. Hence the name. That's the idea, at least. I had certainly used it all the time back in medical school.

The entry on Castleman disease said that there had been only four reported cases of my subtype (idiopathic multicentric)—ever—and in only one of those cases was the patient still alive. I was shocked. One of my resident doctors at Duke and I incorrectly assumed this meant I was the fifth case ever. It was hard to imagine that any effective treatment would have been developed for such a small community. Efforts to develop a cure for a disease with such a small incidence could even be considered by some to be an irresponsible use of limited research resources, though I would not have complained. With the kind of desperation that a shipwreck survivor might lash together a raft, we did some frantic research in the hope that there were more of us—idiopathic multicentric Castleman disease patients—out there. It turned out that a single clinical trial had recently enrolled over seventy-five patients with the idiopathic multicentric subtype of Castleman disease. And a quick search of PubMed revealed that there were actually hundreds of published case reports of this subtype. The UpToDate page was, in fact, not up to date.

I am now the author of the UpToDate page on Castleman disease, so I can tell you that it is up to date. We now know that there are an estimated six to seven thousand individuals diagnosed with Castleman disease *each year* in the United States, which makes this disease about as common as ALS. And about one thousand of those patients are diagnosed with my subtype, iMCD, each year. With an average survival of about seven years for iMCD patients, there are an estimated seven thousand patients alive in the United States. Not one.

But at the time, it was enough to know that there were clinical trials going on. That meant that the disease was rare but not irrelevant. Which meant that I needed to get out of the hematology ward at Duke and find myself an expert. There was bound to be one. I was willing to travel anywhere. These kinds of diseases can often attract the brightest minds, who are drawn to the pursuit of complex and under-studied problems. I would soon dream of joining one of those teams.

Sure enough, after a little digging online, Gena and I found who we were looking for: one Dr. Frits van Rhee, a professor with an MD, a PhD, and distinguished fellowships from a number of international institutions, who received significant research funding from the NIH (the top badge of honor in the research community) to study multiple myeloma, and held a reputation as the foremost expert on Castleman disease anyone could find. He was now down at the University of Arkansas for Medical Sciences.

I emailed Dr. van Rhee to ask if he'd see me in Little Rock once I was healthy enough to be discharged from Duke. I was happy to be going right to the top, but the process brought with it an undeniably grave significance. It was like appealing to the Supreme Court. He was the undisputed authority on what was killing me. I dared not think about the possibility that he didn't have all the answers.

Dr. van Rhee wrote back right away and said that he'd be happy to see me. I decided to interpret his punctuality as a good omen. Anyone that busy but that prompt must have an extra gear.

My appointment with Dr. van Rhee would be on December 26. I'd need to get a PET scan, bone marrow biopsy, and blood work. I'd been at Duke for a month, I'd received last rites and chemotherapy. I wasn't feeling at all well, and my blood work looked terrible. I had just three weeks to build up my strength before traveling to Little Rock and to learn as much as I could about Castleman disease. My story no longer had a fable-like quality of mysterious misery. I was no longer in a heroic saga, being ground down by some unknowable force. In that sense, my story had turned the corner. It was a detective story now, and there was a ticking time bomb buried deep within my body that needed to be defused.

But first I needed some new clothes after discharge. Due to all of the excess fluid, my belly was bigger than my seven-months-pregnant sister's. Nothing I'd owned before this crisis would fit. I wasn't about to just wear hospital gowns everywhere. I still had *some* pride. So my sister and I purchased a number of logo-less XXXL outfits for me to wear. I looked like a mafia don in prison clothes.

I also needed to mend some fences, if I could. The first person I called when I got to my dad's house was Caitlin. Again, I tried to explain why I had turned her away. Again, she accepted my apology, but again, I'd later learn, she thought it had been my sisters protecting me. There were many more emotions and thoughts bubbling below the surface that were not being said— I think we were both just so exhausted from the ups and downs of the last few months. She did reveal more about what it had been like for her during those visits when she couldn't see me. I could feel us getting closer when we spoke. The tension between us faded away, and that old feeling of pure happiness I remembered so well from when we dated took over. But I tried not to think too far ahead about our relationship. Who knew what tomorrow would bring with my awful disease? I tried to just savor it for what it was: a phone call with the woman I loved. To be awake for it.

CHAPTER TEN

IN 1954 A pathologist from Massachusetts first observed a pattern of microscopic irregularities in lymph nodes from about ten patients suffering from similar symptoms. His name was Benjamin Castleman, and this complex disease was named in his honor. But that's where the simplicity of the name ends.

The first clue to the complication at the heart of my disease is how it is named: the *i* of *iMCD* refers to it being "idiopathic." That just means more or less that we don't know what causes it.

As far as we knew when I was diagnosed, iMCD came down to cytokines, those immune cell secretions that do so much to trigger and coordinate the initiatives of the whole system. Well, one cytokine in particular: interleukin-6 or IL-6. Everyone makes and secretes IL-6; you're probably secreting some right now. It helps us to fight off infections and cancer. But, in iMCD, IL-6 production goes into overdrive and doesn't stop—friendly fire run amok—causing flu-like symptoms and life-threatening disturbances to the liver, kidneys, heart, lungs, and bone marrow. Why was it overproduced to start? That's one of the things

we didn't know. Perhaps it was triggered by a particularly ob-
noxious foreign agent like a virus, or perhaps the emergence of
cancer cells set it off. Or perhaps the trigger was endogenous: a
mutation in the genetic code—either programmed from birth
or acquired during the course of life—of an immune cell. No
one knew. So, we didn't even know if iMCD should be called
an autoimmune disease, a cancer, or a virally driven disease. It
defied classification, seeming to act like a cross between the cancer lymphoma and the autoimmune disease lupus and occupy-
ing a no-man's-land between the two.

I also learned that all cases of Castleman disease are not alike
and the subtype—as in cancer—has important implications.
After "idiopathic," my subtype is called "multicentric Castleman
disease," because there are multiple regions of enlarged lymph
nodes that have a microscopic appearance similar to what
Dr. Castleman first described. The lymph nodes are the home
bases for immune cells to get their marching orders: whom to
fight, what to do, and how to avoid damaging healthy cells along
the way. This extremely complex process, which is occurring all
day, every day for every one of us, requires that various immune
cells go to precise locations in the lymph node to give and receive the correct messages. In Castleman disease, the lymph
nodes have blood vessels abnormally traversing everywhere and
immune cells that are packed in an abnormal distribution and,
thus, at risk of receiving incorrect messages that send them out
into the body in attack mode.

There are three other forms of Castleman disease that share
this strange appearance under the microscope. One is unicentric
Castleman disease (UCD), which involves milder symptoms
than iMCD and a single confined region of enlarged lymph
nodes; surgical excision of the nodes is often curative. Another
is POEMS-associated MCD, where a small number of cancerous cells cause clinical and laboratory abnormalities just like in
iMCD. Eliminating those cancerous cells abrogates the MCD.

The last is human herpesvirus 8 (HHV-8)–associated MCD, which also involves a syndrome almost identical to iMCD, but it is caused by uncontrolled infection with the HHV-8 virus. Research is quite advanced for this subtype. Before the cause and key immune cell types had been worked out, HHV-8-associated MCD had an even worse prognosis than iMCD. Now that the cause and mechanisms of HHV-8-associated MCD have been untangled, effective treatments have led to significant improvements in long-term survival. The take-home message for me: My form of the disease wasn't invincible if we could just uncover what was underlying it.

But even buoyed by this insight, I found the data on survival tough to read. As with multiple system organ failure, what I had theoretically understood in medical school about survival data now took on a new and personal meaning. About 35 percent of iMCD patients die within five years of diagnosis. This is identical to the average survival rate when you combine all cancers together and worse than lymphoma, bladder cancer, breast cancer, multiple sclerosis, and prostate cancer. And about 60 percent of iMCD patients die within ten years of diagnosis. Unlike many of those other terrible diseases, iMCD can be diagnosed at any age, so children and young adults are also often in this battle against the odds.

I scanned papers multiple times to find any clues about the cause, the immune cell types, or the cellular communication lines primarily involved in my disease. Five and a half decades had passed since Dr. Castleman reported the first case, but the cause, key cell types, and key cellular communication lines were all unknown; the only breakthrough was the finding that IL-6 production is in overdrive, which came from a few studies of a few iMCD patients. But an issue in medicine is that you can see only what you look for. Of the hundreds of known cytokines, IL-6 was one of the few that had ever been measured in iMCD, so there could have been other important cytokines that just hadn't been measured. Nevertheless, a drug called tocilizumab, which blocks the receptor for IL-6, was approved for the treatment of iMCD in Japan based on its efficacy in a portion of patients. But it never met the thresholds for efficacy, safety, and rigorous study design demanded by the FDA for approval for iMCD treatment in the United States. However, it *was* eventually approved for the treatment of rheumatoid arthritis in the United States, and thus available if my doctors at Duke had wanted to try it and if they could have gotten insurance approval. But they hadn't known about it.

And at this early stage in my own Castleman disease education and research, I didn't know about the use of tocilizumab for iMCD in Japan either. All I knew was that Castleman disease was an amazingly complex and indisputably fascinating disease. Separate from the misery it inflicted, the disease—as well as we knew it—was a marvel, and the ability of my immune system to attack my organs was awesome, in a way.

Right around the same time that I was trying to learn as much as I could about iMCD to help myself, researchers were leveraging some of what had been learned about cytokines in iMCD to fight cancer. This is one of the seminal achievements of medicine: our ability to learn from threats to our health, and our shamelessness in copying weapons from our enemies in order to fire back.

For cancer, the hope and plan is to carefully direct the immune system's firepower at the cancer itself (and the cancer only). Of course there are risks. Unleashing these powerful weapons and pointing them in the "wrong" direction means that patients often get sicker before they get better. Over the last two decades, colleagues of mine at the University of Pennsylvania and elsewhere have figured out ways to reprogram specialized killer immune cells, called T cells, to target and kill cancer cells that are expressing certain molecules on their surface. They do this by removing T cells from the patient and actually harnessing components of the HIV virus to insert genetic material into these cells. Once the cells, called chimeric antigen receptor or CAR T cells, are reinfused, they go on a killing spree, releasing cytokines and activating the immune system to destroy cancer cells displaying specific cellular markers. Not surprisingly, these patients often get very sick, very quickly. In fact, one of the first patients ever treated with CAR T cells was dying in the ICU with symptoms, organ dysfunction, and immune hyperactivation almost identical to iMCD. Her IL-6 levels were off the charts. The doctors decided to try tocilizumab, the IL-6 receptor-blocking drug originally developed for the treatment of iMCD in Japan.

It worked. Had her life not been saved by tocilizumab, the entire CAR T cell research program may have been shut down. Today, CAR T cell therapies are FDA-approved for treating multiple types of leukemia and lymphoma and are the latest hope in the moon shot fight against many other cancers too.

There's a sense in the public that these so-called miracle drugs are popping up every day and that the medical field has the answers to nearly everything that ails us. Much of this sense comes from the fact that we hear about only the "breakthroughs" in the media. Headlines don't say, "One hundred thousand laboratory experiments did not result in a single breakthrough today." Many believe that these "miracles" just happen, and they fall into the researchers' laps. That's certainly not true. Tocilizumab is a case in point. Dr. Kazuyuki Yoshizaki, who first discovered elevated IL-6 in a few iMCD patients and spent more than a decade developing tocilizumab for the treatment of iMCD back in the 1990s and 2000s, tried it on himself before administering it to any other humans in an experimental clinical trial. He wanted to prove it was safe. When I asked him about it, he laughed, pointed to his arm, and said, "No, no, no. I didn't administer it to myself. The nurse, she administered it to me."

Kazu isn't the first medical researcher to experiment on himself, or the last. In fact, twelve Nobel Prizes have been given to self-experimenters. Dr. Werner Forssmann pioneered the development of cardiac catheterization by first inserting such a catheter into a vein in his arm and successfully guiding it to his heart. Dr. Barry Marshall proved that a particular strain of bacteria causes ulcers by drinking a broth filled with the bacteria. This led to a Nobel Prize and also an entirely new way of treating—and curing—such ulcers.

Kazu's example—that of both scientist and subject—would come to be very, very significant for me.

As I researched Castleman disease, I felt a part of me reemerging, a part I had had to lay down when I first dragged myself into the ER: I felt like a doctor again. Some of that identity no longer wore as well as it once did. *As* a doctor, I had been trained to look at disease as the sum of the parts that fit into our diagnostic tools. We were trained, rightly, to attend to what we could fix, and what we could fix only. When I became a patient, the deficiencies of this straitened approach revealed themselves to me. I began to understand what Susan Sontag meant when she said that each of us is born with dual citizenship, ultimately obliged to spend some time in the Kingdom of the Sick. My disease *wasn't* just the sum of its symptoms; it became a relationship I had to the world, and to the people around me.

I was very much a citizen of that kingdom one day in North Carolina, seven days before we were scheduled to leave for Arkansas, when my sister Lisa patiently helped me go to the mall to walk some laps. There were no other "walkers" that I could see; the place was packed with Christmas shoppers. I had been discharged from Duke a couple weeks earlier, and I was in a good stretch, eager to improve my fitness. I was sporting one of my new XXXL gray sweat suits to try to cover my distended belly, still full of about five liters of fluid, and my feet were too swollen to fit into any shoes, so I wore hospital socks and Adidas sandals with the Velcro straps adjusted to maximum width.

I looked like I had just escaped from Nurse Ratched. But I didn't care. I *felt* great.

I rounded a corner and briefly made eye contact with a woman about my age. I smiled and had reason to hope for a smile in return. In case you've never spent time in the South, let me tell you that it's a truth undiminished by cliché: People smile back. But this woman not only didn't smile, she gave me a look of absolute revulsion. Lisa caught the brief exchange, and she and I burst into laughter. For a brief moment I had forgotten that I was in the kingdom . . . And to laugh felt so good. I guess I no longer looked like the Beast of before, but more like I'd been attacked by one.

Our family celebrated Christmas together, and it felt even more special than it had in all of the years since my mom had died. But I still couldn't get my mind off what I really wanted from Santa: for Dr. van Rhee to give me my health back.

When we finally arrived in Little Rock the next day, we got into a shuttle at the airport and said we were going to the University of Arkansas for Medical Sciences. The driver asked, "Is it for Castleman disease?"

I was completely shocked. "Yes."

"I thought you looked like you might be a Castleman disease patient."

It had taken doctors at top medical centers eleven weeks to figure out I had Castleman disease, but the shuttle driver got it at hello.

"Well, you're in the right place. Dr. van Rhee takes care of Castleman disease patients from around the world."

This was comforting. For the first time, I was going to a place where what I had was *normal*.

The same thing happened when we checked in to our hotel and when we walked into the clinic. Everyone we met seemed

to know about Castleman disease. I had just been at a top medical center where specialist physicians didn't know anything
about Castleman disease and the top medical resource in the
world erroneously said there was only one patient reported to
be alive with my subtype. I could definitely say, now, that this
wasn't true, since there was a line of iMCD patients waiting to
see Dr. van Rhee that morning. I was finally in the right place.

I'd come prepared. Like all good obsessives, I'd put together
a PowerPoint to track my initial differential diagnosis as well as
symptoms and lab tests for the last few months. The report had
ballooned to over one hundred pages, and when I shared it with
Dr. van Rhee I was nervous he might roll his eyes and look at
his watch—here I was, a patient, a medical student, supposing to
educate the master. But that wasn't his approach at all. Instead,
he spent three hours with my dad and me to review the data and
come up with a detailed treatment plan. As we talked, we discovered that we had more than an interest in Castleman disease
in common: His wife is from Trinidad and grew up in the same
neighborhood as my mom. We reminisced about the island, our
favorite Trini foods, and our favorite beaches.

Those shared cultural touch points were comforting, but the
most encouraging part was that what he was proposing represented the sum total of the world's knowledge on my illness.
It—and he—was amazing. He informed us that a pharmaceutical company was studying a drug called siltuximab, which
blocked IL-6 directly, as a treatment for iMCD,* and it was already in Phase II of clinical trials—the first Phase II, randomized
controlled study of iMCD ever. If it was successful, the FDA
would likely approve siltuximab for use in iMCD. Early reports
were really encouraging. I was shocked to learn that the clinical
trial was enrolling patients just fifteen minutes down the road

---

* Tocilizumab and siltuximab both inhibit the IL-6 signaling pathway. Tocilizumab blocks the receptor for IL-6 from binding with IL-6. Siltuximab binds
directly to and neutralizes IL-6.

from Duke, at the University of North Carolina, and neither I nor my doctors had been aware of it when I was dying there. My own IL-6 levels had not been elevated when they were tested during my initial presentation and relapse, but Dr. van Rhee explained that, based on what's known about iMCD, I must have elevated IL-6—it's a critical component of iMCD. He went on that the test for IL-6 is not very good, so it was likely falsely low. Our plan was for me to return to North Carolina to enroll in the siltuximab clinical trial. It was the only drug in clinical trials for iMCD and it directly targeted a critical factor in the disease. This, finally, was what I'd been hoping for. Expertise, plans, and action. I was elated.

At the end of our appointment, Dr. van Rhee walked me down the hall to meet another patient, a man about my age with iMCD who'd also spent months in critical condition in an ICU and then nearly died again when he relapsed. He had experienced multiple strokes and had a large portion of his colon resected and was now nearly back to 100 percent thanks to the same experimental drug that Dr. van Rhee had recommended for me. He put a face on my future, and it made me more hopeful than I had been in months. I was going back home, but this time I was armed and dangerous. No more passive hope.

That was the plan, at least. We got in a cab the following day to go to the airport. Between the moment we stepped into the cab and the moment we stepped out, I realized I was relapsing. The fatigue and nausea had been worsening over the previous couple of days, but between my visit with Dr. van Rhee and finally having a plan, I avoided connecting the dots. Then it started hitting me hard. At the airport, to confirm my hunch, I pulled up a website with the results of blood tests performed at van Rhee's clinic. There was no question. My body and my blood told me everything.

Round three was starting.

We left the terminal, got back in a cab, and returned to the hospital. I was disappointed and scared. But, hey, at least I was in the Mecca for Castleman disease, I thought to myself.

Dr. van Rhee immediately admitted me and started me on higher doses of the same corticosteroids that had saved my life at Rex and a double dose of the chemotherapy that had saved my life at Duke.

Within a few days, it was clear that they would not be effective this time around. My Castleman disease was roaring.

I was quickly started on dialysis to replace the function of my failing kidneys. I received multiple blood, platelet, and albumin transfusions, every day. They pulled six to seven liters of fluid out of my abdomen a few times a week. My body became a site of coming and going, taking and leaving, stopping and starting, and failing.

The clinical trial that Dr. van Rhee wanted me to enroll in required an eight-week period without any other treatments before starting. That way you know that any observed improvements are due to the siltuximab. My doctors and I knew that I couldn't survive that long without treatment, so Dr. van Rhee appealed to the FDA and the drug company for emergency compassionate use to allow me to receive the experimental treatment even though I couldn't enroll in the formal clinical trial. Considering my grave illness and lack of options, they granted the request.

I received the first dose and hoped. During my infusion, a clinical trial coordinator told my dad and me about how she had seen patients experience dramatic turnarounds within just a couple of days. She and my nurse explained that if my IL-6 level began to rise very high after siltuximab was given, that would be a sign that the drug was going to work for me.

Two days went by and my condition continued to worsen.

I felt no improvement, and my lab tests confirmed that things were getting worse.

My organs continued to fail.

And then finally the sign that we'd all been hoping for! The level of IL-6 in my blood was now more than one hundred times greater than normal. My nurse and trial coordinator reminded me that this indicated that the siltuximab should start working soon.

So my dad and I celebrated with a high five, and he called family and friends to share the news. Then, we waited for my miraculous turnaround to occur.

Two more days passed. My organ function deteriorated even further, and I began to lose consciousness again. One of my doctors informed me that we couldn't wait any longer for the drug to work. I was approaching the point of no return.

The miracle drug had come. It targeted the one thing "known" about the disease: IL-6 was the problem, and yet blocking it hadn't worked. No other drugs were being studied.

Though my thoughts were foggy—my brain was also suffering from the multiple system organ failure—I was still provoked by the intellectual problem: Why hadn't blocking IL-6 worked the way we'd all expected? What was different about me? I understood that it was unlikely I was going to live long enough to ever know the answers to those questions.

Dr. van Rhee came by my room to discuss what to do next. During our brief chat, we both reasoned that maybe the siltuximab was actually working and that I would be even more sick without it or maybe it was just going to take more time than we had for it to start working. After he left, I thought to myself that perhaps my samples would be useful to Dr. van Rhee's research in the future and to future patients like me. But there in the hospital, the pressing matter wasn't research. It was keeping me from flatlining. There was nothing left to do but fight fire with fire.

Dr. van Rhee decided to initiate the closest thing to a "shock and awe" campaign on my disease—a combination of massive, obliterating doses of seven chemotherapy drugs that is known by the initials of its ingredients: Velcade, dexamethasone, thalido-mide, Adriamycin, cyclophosphamide, etoposide, and ritux-imab. The worst components of VDT-ACER would be deployed continuously for the first four days. Then, agents tar-geted at specific and strategic aspects of the immune system would be administered every couple of days for the next seven-teen. The regimen was originally developed to treat multiple myeloma, a blood cancer with similarities to iMCD, and had never actually been studied in iMCD. The team dutifully warned me about the side effects that I'd endure, but I told them to bring it on. I knew what to expect, at least by the book. The toxicity was off the charts. They said my hair would fall out, they said I would be constantly vomiting, and they said this might prevent me from being able to have children.

My hair fell out. I vomited, frequently. I wasn't ready to give up on the possibility of children in my future, but I needed to survive this if I was going to have a chance. My father sat by my bed and encouraged me to eat crackers.

The obscene thing was: I felt better with every new dose of chemotherapy. The iMCD flare-ups were so all-consumingly awful that the semicontrolled poisoning of VDT-ACER was an improvement. My brain was still cloudy, and moving most of my body still wasn't possible. But every step in the right direc-tion felt amazing even if it was gradual. I was benefiting from one of the greatest of all aspects of human psychology: habitua-tion. Anything felt better after escaping from hell.

The drugs were killing my immune system, which had been trying to kill me. It was a temporary fix, but that's all I could expect until someone could crack the iMCD code.

In the meantime, I had a new appreciation for the drugs that I'd spent my whole medical education learning about. They'd always just been tools in the tool kit of the physician. But now I got it: Drugs save lives. Doctors administer them.

Don't mistake me—I think doctors are the catalytic element,

but drugs are the underlying material. This will piss off some doctors, I know. I would have been pissed off by this thinking back before my own journey. In the medical community, there is often a resistance to acknowledging the primacy of drugs and I think that this resistance can sow confusion. In a very real way, the drugs available to us represent the hard limits of what we can do for patients. Of course, when to use and when *not* to use a treatment is a highly complex decision and requires the special insight of a great doctor, but you can't target something if a drug doesn't exist to target it.

Whether it was a side effect of all those wonderful drugs, or just the need to unburden myself after coming back from near death for a third time, I strangely felt the urge to confess to my dad about each of the times that I had lied to him while I was growing up. It was now about six months since I first became sick, and he had been sleeping in a pullout chair, by my side, every night. Maybe I felt like he deserved hearing the truth after all he had done for me. Maybe I felt like I needed to get everything off my chest in case I took a turn for the worst; maybe I figured I was still in such bad shape he wouldn't get mad at me about anything. Whatever triggered it, I confessed to a lot of "borrowing" the car when he was out of town and ignoring sensible advice. He forgave me.

He also gave me privacy so I could call Caitlin from my room. Once again, she and I began to reconnect, filling each other in on the details of our day-to-day lives. I infused all of my energy into what became weekly calls. Though my updates for her were decidedly less upbeat, I loved hearing about even the mundane details of her life at work. She had taken a job in New York in the fashion industry after college, and it made us both laugh to think that anyone could consider an incorrect stitch or unexpected shade of green to be a life-or-death mistake. We knew better!

On New Year's Eve, I felt well enough to walk laps around the hematology/oncology floor with my dad by my side. I had a belly that protruded about as far as my now eight-months-pregnant sister's, and I wore a mask to limit my risk of developing an infection, since my immune system was weakened—intentionally and fortunately—from all that chemotherapy. As we rounded a corner near the family waiting area, we noticed a man who showed every sign of having been drinking that evening. It was New Year's Eve after all. On our next lap, we saw that he had fallen out of his chair and was lying on the floor. My dad, ever the doctor, rushed over to help him back up. The man slurred out his thanks and then added, "Good luck to you and your wife." We continued on, confused, until I looked down and realized that due to my protruding belly (and, I hope, the man's intoxication), I must have looked like I was nine months pregnant and we were walking laps to speed our delivery. He thought I was my dad's pregnant wife! I couldn't resist telling my dad: "Man, you've got an ugly wife." We were soon doubled over with laughter.

Death isn't funny, of course. But I came to understand that in no situation other than facing death is a sense of humor more necessary.

It could have been bleak as hell to be so grotesquely twisted and transformed by my organ failures that I was misgendered by a drunk. That could easily be rock bottom in a different story, told by a different person. It might well have been rock bottom for me before I got repeatedly sick. After all, I was once full of pride and competitive spirit, and capable of 375-pound bench presses; I won't pretend that I never cared about how I looked.

And not that much time had passed since very similar conditions had made me act very differently. I wasn't laughing when I turned Caitlin away because of fear that my appearance would be burned into her memory. That wasn't funny. It won't ever be.

What was different then, that day in the hospital with my dad?

I was different.

In my doctor role, I'd seen astonishing instances of patients in terrible circumstances still seeing the essential comedy in their conditions. I'd always just chalked it up to a kind of avoidance. People are geniuses at turning away from what's in front of them. Humor seemed to work that way.

Now I knew that I'd had it all wrong. Humor didn't let me avoid anything. It made me look my suffering in the eye—and laugh at it. Facing my horrible moments with laughter was just as fundamentally a rejection of Castleman's dominion over me as anything else I was doing. It cleared my mind; it stiffened my resolve. It was entirely up to me to determine what was and what wasn't funny. Perhaps most important, humor is social. For me and my family, there was never a better way to reset our collective resolve than laughing together. My mom had first taught me this when we laughed together as she did donuts in that grocery store scooter. Now my dad and I shared a moment like this too.

After seven weeks of multiagent chemotherapy, daily transfusions, and frequent dialysis sessions, I was well enough for discharge. Just before we left, I told one of my favorite nurses, Norm, how much I couldn't wait to get out. "I've been in hospitals for most of the last six months," I added. My dad, who was sitting beside me just as he'd been for the last six months, interrupted and said, "What is this '*I've* been in the hospital'? *We've* been in the hospital!" It was true, and I'd clearly taken his presence for granted—he'd canceled all surgeries and office appointments for the last six months and slept in my hospital room nearly every night; only when my sister Lisa came to visit did he go to a nearby hotel to sleep in a bed. And he was always back first thing in the morning. His was a thankless job—bearing quiet and worried witness to his

Davey Boy's plight day after day. My energy level and optimism often rose when friends and other family members came by—my godparents and their son Conner, who was like a brother to me, were rejuvenating visitors. But when they left, my own energy and optimism would tank. And my father would be there to bear that too.

Home to North Carolina we went. I'd won round three, but it was a TKO. The miracle drug we'd pinned our hopes on—the IL-6 blocker siltuximab—hadn't worked, and we'd had to call in an all-out chemo strike. Even still, Dr. van Rhee (and I) reasoned that maybe I was just too sick for siltuximab to work by the time we started using it. Maybe my IL-6 levels had actually been very high when the test results previously came back normal, maybe they were just not being detected by the IL-6 test. We thought and hoped that siltuximab might still work to prevent another relapse even if it wasn't able to stop a relapse in its tracks. After all, it supposedly had wonder-like powers in treating iMCD. I left Dr. van Rhee's office with a plan written out on a piece of yellow paper: siltuximab every three weeks.

The uneasiness I felt, even leaving Arkansas with my health returning to me, was this: We'd been ramping up our counterattacks each round—but there was nothing more powerful left in the arsenal. Also, just as much as iMCD was a ticking time bomb, these drugs were creating another. A human body can take the onslaught of such toxic chemotherapy only so many times before the damage is too great, the so-called lifetime max dose. Most patients never get to that point, where the heart and other vital organs are too damaged to keep going or a cancer is spawned *because of* the DNA damage caused by the chemotherapy intended to kill the disease. If chemotherapy was my only solution to a relapse, how many more episodes did I have left before the chemo itself killed me? But I kept these thoughts at bay. Instead, I reminded myself: Siltuximab was going to keep me in remission. Plus, I had the top expert in the field caring for me. I just knew that he and teams of others must have been working on figuring out the mysteries of iMCD; it wouldn't be "idiopathic" for long, I thought. But solving those mysteries didn't really matter for me, because I was on the miracle drug for my disease. It wouldn't come back.

CHAPTER ELEVEN

AS SOON AS I got to the airport back home in Raleigh, I did something I hadn't done in ten years: I sat down at Five Guys and had a hamburger.

I hadn't eaten any form of ground meat in a decade. I had also carefully removed the skin from every piece of chicken, and I hadn't had fried foods or any fat-filled additive like mayo or butter either. I'd been a model of clean eating, filling my plate with fruits, vegetables, fish, (skinless) chicken, and whole grains. Dried mango slices were my splurge food. In the name of good health (and some amount of vanity), I had tamped down the urge to eat for joy; "I don't eat for taste," I'd once proudly declared to my friends while itemizing the calorie count and grams of protein on the plate in front of me. Even still, I had now nearly died several times—and it was hard to keep up the pretense that food was the culprit. Indeed, my own well-nourished body had turned on itself. I'm not sure if it was my realization that pristine nutrition can take you only so far toward the uncertain state of good health (a "stronger" immune system was actually the last thing I needed) or the fact that I'd been fed through a feeding tube for weeks, but as I walked through that airport, my carnivorism was reawakened. I no longer saw the wisdom in cutting off a channel to joy.

I savored that hamburger. It was like a feast after a long, abstemious Lent—or that first solid meal after you have the flu.

Sitting down and eating it also gave me a moment of quiet to think about something I'd been mulling over the past few weeks: a new orientation for a new phase in my battle for life (or my victory lap phase, as I thought of it—wrongly—then). I was envisioning a new modus operandi. *Think it, do it* kept reeling through my mind. The comma was important. It was not a full stop. Not thinking of some things *and* doing some other things haphazardly but thinking of some things, *then* doing those same things, and there was no stopping halfway through.

I didn't—and still don't—see this new mantra as an excuse to be impulsive; I wasn't planning to blurt out exactly what was on my mind, or manically start buying things online. *Think it, do it* has developed into a guiding principle of sorts. Don't just let thoughts come and go. Every thought should be broken down and evaluated to determine if it's worth doing. If so, then it's go mode—whether or not you have all the ideal skills to do it. This has made me more scrupulous about *what* I really want, and *which* thoughts actually warrant doing. It's made me more economical about what I spend mental energy on, yet ironically it also helps me banish the doubting hobgoblin I have living in the back of my mind. We often think of doing things or saying things that would have a material impact on our own lives or the lives of those we love but quickly talk ourselves out of them. *Think it, do it* helped me to cull useless thoughts, and to elevate those worth doing. Eating a hamburger that day felt like the latter.

I'd started piecing together this new orientation back in Arkansas, during the first days of smooth sailing after the worst of

my third brush with death. It came from the very simple realization that the regrets that ate at me the most as I prepared to die
weren't about anything I'd done; my greatest regrets were things
that I had thought of doing but never did. I know I'm not the
first to come to this conclusion: "No one on their deathbed ever
wishes they'd spent more time at the office" is a cliché because
it's true. When you're healthy, the things that keep you up at
night are memories: the stupid joke you told at the dinner party,
the bad pass, the time you told the girl you loved her . . . on the
second date. Memories you'd rather not have, but memories
nonetheless. But when you're dying—or at least when I was
dying—these memories become quite insignificant. It's the absence of memories that you wish you had made and the realization that you'll never get the chance to make them that coalesce
into a horribly vivid pit of regret in your stomach (and trigger
the alarm for a rapid heart rate on your ICU monitor). I must
have imagined marriage and kids with Caitlin a hundred times,
half in delirium and half in agony. And wished that I had at least
fought for our relationship or gotten back together when she
gave me the chance so we could have had what I thought were
my final six months together. I grieved for memories that didn't
exist. I told myself that if I made it, I'd do everything in my
power to make sure my thoughts turned into actions.

That night we had a family feast. We had lots to celebrate: I was
home, and Gena had had a second healthy daughter while I'd
been in Little Rock. Everyone came to my dad's house for dinner. I was too weak to lift even a bowl of food, let alone cook
or ferry serving dishes to the table, but I helped out by setting
the table. It was the most joyful table setting of all time. Martha
Stewart couldn't have done better. I smiled ear to ear as I folded
the napkins precisely into perfect triangles and studiously
counted my every blessing.

Buoyed by the evening's happiness, I decided to quiet the hobgoblin in my head and get on with "doing." I called Caitlin. We had talked periodically on the phone while I was in Arkansas, and just that afternoon (after my insight-inspiring hamburger), I had sent her her favorite flowers and what I remembered to be her favorite candy at her office. The act was in no way heroic, but the action was significant. My internal naysayer had tried every which way to talk me out of sending the gifts. *You're not even dating, she'll think it's weird, just wait to do something else some other time.* These thoughts had typically won out earlier in my life. Now, though, enlightened by my ICU experience and new motto, I just did it.

But I couldn't fool myself into thinking anything was settled—showing that I remembered her flower and candy preferences was a nice first step, but it couldn't begin to undo the damage I'd done by twice refusing her at my deathbed. Now, I plucked up the courage and asked if she'd visit me in Raleigh. She agreed. I took her willingness to travel to see me as a good sign, but I found plenty of reasons to worry anyway. Even though I was getting better, I still had a belly filled with seven liters of fluid, and I was bald from the chemotherapy (some people can rock that look; I . . . cannot). My appearance was all that I could think about. I was fixated on it. But of course, my disfigured body was the tip of the proverbial iceberg—it was what I could see of the Castleman disease and a reminder of the much more troubling issues below the surface. The Castleman disease was out of sight and out of mind for the time being. My looks were definitively not.

It had been more than a year since we had seen each other in person. I worried about the first fumbling, awkward moments, and I worried about what came after them. To be frank, I worried that Caitlin wouldn't want to get back together given all I was going through and all I had put her through. That would be understandable. It would be awful, but understandable.

Still, I was going to try. I was thinking it, now I was doing it.

Caitlin got to Raleigh a few weeks later and came right to my sister's house. This time I didn't tell her to stay outside or talk to her through an intermediary. I met her at the door. She saw me. I saw her seeing me. After visiting with my sister and my niece whom Caitlin had spent years babysitting, Caitlin and I had our first moments alone sitting on my sister's couch, a couch that we'd spent so much time on together when we were dating.

I had one hand on Caitlin's shoulder and the other on my head in a futile attempt to hide the baldness.

But she wasn't thinking about my appearance. She had something else on her mind: She told me that she wanted us to get back together.

"Are you sure?" I said as I looked away. I didn't want to make eye contact, I didn't want to betray how bad I wanted this. I needed her to make the decision herself, independent of what I wanted.

When you get sick, it's nice when people act out of sympathy. It's great when people take care of you, and bring you comfort. When you get very, very sick, it's . . . no longer always as nice. You worry that they are doing what they are doing for you out of a sense of obligation or fear of your imminent demise. I'm sure most of the time most people can't untangle their motivations even if they try; they are simply doing what they are moved to do. But as the beneficiary of that kindness or attention, you start to worry about what people would have done in the absence of your condition. You know that they are being themselves, yes, but they are also responding to you in the face of your disease. That means that you are no longer just you, the person they might be happy or angry with, the person they might have hugged or shouted at under different (healthy) circumstances. Instead, you are now and perhaps forever a person with a disease. And that means that what people are willing to do for you or however they might be willing to sacrifice their own needs is now predicated—consciously or not—at least a little on your illness.

Don't get me wrong, I wanted to be in this world as a team with Caitlin, together again, more than anything. But I also ached and felt guilty for the decision she was facing. I saw her choices as to throw her lot in with someone for whom there might not be much of a future or to walk away and perhaps carry the ache herself of knowing that she had disappointed a (possibly) dying man.

But I know now that my health had little or nothing to do with what she'd decided she wanted for us. Instead, she'd been wrestling with whether or not I might change the frenetic pace at which I'd been chasing my ambitions and whether she could live with it if I didn't. She'd been thinking about how she and I could make each other the top priority in our respective lives and how she would feel if she decided not to find out whether it was possible. That I was so sick accelerated her desire to get on with trying. Pitying me or not wanting to let a sick man down had nothing to do with it.

I sat there, still afraid to meet her gaze. She waited for me to finally look up, then gave me a look I'll never forget: It was "Are you crazy?" and "I am sure" all at once.

"But I'm so fat and bald!" I protested kind of weakly. She held my eyes and didn't waver, though she added an eyebrow raise that told me that assuming she was put off by my physical state was actually kind of insulting.

So I got to the root of the issue: "Caitlin, who knows when this thing might come back again?"

"*Who cares?*" she said emphatically.

And that was that. With those two words, she secured two

things for me: (1) my happiness, and (2) my knowledge that her love was unconditional. I now realize that very few people my age are lucky enough to experience this security, the sure knowledge that she would be with me through thick and thin, fatness and baldness, through terrible times, and more. Before she left on that Sunday to return to New York, we made a plan to visit each other as much as we could. Her busy work schedule and my frailty meant that visits wouldn't be as often as we'd like, but it felt good to have a plan.

In the weeks and months to come, I would have to emphasize again that my sisters had, in fact, been doing exactly what I'd repeatedly asked them to do. And I had to try to explain my somewhat twisted logic: Denying Caitlin access to me was actually the highest form of prioritization I could think of. I truly thought I was doing the right thing in preserving her memories of me as a fully alive and healthy man.

I would come to understand that my imagination had been limited. The highest form of prioritization would have been to allow myself to be fully vulnerable in her presence.

When I had strung together five weeks of good health, my longest period out of a hospital in seven months, I was eager to believe I'd beaten this thing after all. That was temporarily a terrific feeling—but it also made me put aside my burgeoning investigation into my disease. Castleman disease was in my rearview mirror, I thought. There were more pressing things: I could finally get up and begin exercising again.

Of course, I had to start small. I began with laps around the kitchen and living room. Not exactly thrilling stuff, but I added spice by playing my favorite walking song on repeat, a weird Soviet-era song I found on YouTube apparently called "Trololo." I recently learned that the actual title roughly translates into "I am very glad, because I'm finally back home"—which couldn't have been more fitting. But the underlying meaning wasn't why I listened to it over and over again. The beat perfectly matched my slow strides as I was building back my strength, and it was great to sing along to. After months of deconditioning, these laps raised my heart rate, made me laugh, and kept me going. That was enough for now.

I didn't neglect my muscles. Soon I was pumping those little two-pound weights you see in senior centers. My four-year-old niece, Anne Marie, was unimpressed. She took the weights out of my hands and showed me that she could do . . . exactly what I was doing. She also took to copying me in another way: She started wearing hats, just as I was doing to hide my baldness and then my patchily regrowing hair. It was heartwarming to have a judgment-free little disciple, someone who looked up to me and followed my lead. But I was clearly no longer the Beast I had once been.

I still had the Beast in my heart, though. And I had a ready store of memories from my football days—when I courted pain, pushed through it, and gained strength from the ordeal—to help me push through. Like the time I was made to roll as fast as I could on an icy football field in subfreezing temperatures until I threw up—well, until everyone threw up—as a punishment for being late to an off-season workout. I hated it at the time, but now I wondered where I'd be if I'd never had the repeated opportunities to face up to agony within the controlled space of the gridiron and weight room. Those experiences were in my bank, and they were paying dividends as I worked my way back from zero. As my weights increased, I took pictures of myself every week to document my transformation. I went from looking pregnant and famished to looking less pregnant and more Beastish.

It was a strange quirk of my disease and recovery that my diminished state actually opened up opportunities where I wouldn't have found them otherwise. Without football or college or graduate school or medical school (I was now on medical leave), I'd never had so much time to devote to the AMF support network as I did now. I dove back into running its operations from our small office in Raleigh, just down the street from Rex Hospital. This was such a gift. I wanted to expand the network to reach even more grieving students around the country. At that time, we had chapters holding support group meetings and community service events on over one hundred college campuses. But I wanted us to help more people. I thought about writing a book to reach all of the students where there were no AMF chapters. Since I thought it, I had to do it. I partnered with a friend and mentor, Dr. Heather Servaty-Seib, to write the book, and we eventually published it with input and stories from grieving young adults in our network. I felt like I was channeling my mother by making a silver lining in my forced downtime.

For six months, I recuperated in Raleigh. I had to go to the hospital every three weeks for my infusion of siltuximab, but I had been getting stronger ever since the Little Rock carpet bombing. And my blood tests had all returned to normal. Things had also changed in a more profound way: Caitlin and I were developing a balanced relationship for the first time . . . ever. Even with so much geographic distance between us. I wasn't burying myself in my work anymore in a way that excluded everyone else and forced me to choose between Caitlin and AMF or Caitlin and medical school. I was choosing balance. And she started volunteering more for AMF, so we could spend time working together to pursue our shared passion for helping grieving college students. We were able to combine and intertwine our lives like never before. And it was so much fun.

By July 2011, I decided it was time to pick up some of the final pieces of my life that Castleman disease had broken apart. That meant going back to medical school and refocusing on training to become an oncologist, which I could not wait to do. And that meant handing the reins of AMF to a full-time and paid executive director. I was proud of how far the organization had come, and I wanted to find the right steward to carry forward what Caitlin, Ben, Lisa, Gena, a number of other volunteers, and I had built. A conversation with one candidate for the job was particularly memorable. He told me that he'd been inspired to apply after reading a book called *Halftime,* which was all about finding significance in the "second half" of your life; he was in his mid-sixties.

"You're too young to read it," he said. "You're not even close to halftime. You're just getting started."

I rubbed my head, which was beginning to sprout back hair, and replied, "I'm in overtime, buddy."

I think, technically, I was in triple OT by that point. Three times I'd seen the clock tick down to zero. Three times I'd been able to get up and get back in the game.

I'd played in plenty of overtimes in football games going all the way back to peewee, and the accumulation of those experiences had taught me something about last-ditch efforts and final attempts. There's a condition of overtime that looks a whole lot like randomness from the outside. The buzzer beater gets clipped and shared online, or the Hail Mary gets on SportsCenter, and it looks so *lucky*. Weird last-second plays get immortalized and celebrated for their rarity. These moments certainly have near-magical potential to transform: One second a basketball coach is sweating, stuck in place, tracking the movement of a ball toward the hoop, and the next . . . he's deliriously racing around the court, looking for someone to hug.

But there's really nothing at all lucky or random or weird or magical about being inside one of those moments. Regardless of outcome, the experience of being in overtime is surprisingly one of intense awareness and scrutiny. And clarity. There's a reason for that: When there are only a few seconds left on the board, all distractions disappear and the purpose—victory—becomes clear. The present is only the things around you, and overtime is all present. Nothing but present and purpose. Over-

time is going back on the field even though you're exhausted.
It's the grass beneath your feet, and the ball in your hands, the
cornerback rocking on his heels, the sun dipping below the stadium bleachers. You know that overtime is overwhelmingly significant. The dropped pass in the second quarter was a bad break
that can be overcome. The dropped pass in overtime is the end
of the game.

That feeling was now with me, 24/7. Every second counted.
Everything needed to have a purpose. That's not to say everything was *fine*. Heck, we still didn't even know what Castleman
disease really was. I hadn't played a perfect game—not even
close—but I understood that you don't end up in overtime or
triple overtime by playing a perfect game. And setbacks can be
just as inspiring. Going blind due to a retinal hemorrhage, receiving poisonous chemotherapy, and feeling the fatigue that
attends organ failure motivated me just as much as waking up,
coming back, and seeing the people I loved again.

In football, every second of overtime contains three
possibilities—one perfect move that means victory, one awful
misstep that means defeat, and a draw that means one more shot
at another moment of overtime. Every second of my life was
now filled with the same three possibilities: triumph, failure, or
getting by. I was hurting, but metaphorically limping off the
field and icing my aching body wasn't in the cards. Surprisingly,
living in overtime liberated me to be my best self.

I returned to medical school in September 2011, but my life
wasn't totally "back to normal" and likely never would be. I still
needed to get infusions of my experimental treatment, siltuximab, every three weeks. That was just a condition of my life
now. I accepted it. I'd seen plenty of patients accept far more
intrusive realities into their lives, and I would have accepted

much worse if it meant that Castleman disease wouldn't come back.

A surprising part of getting seriously ill and getting better is discovering how profoundly expensive *normal* can be. In trying to reengineer a (mostly) normal life for myself, I ran quickly into the real costs of things I'd taken for granted—such as being able to be away from the hospital. My treatment had to be administered back in North Carolina, and school was in Philadelphia, so I was going to have to take thirty-four flights a year. For who knew how long. When I told my friend Ryan about what I was facing, he jumped into action, organizing a party in New York City to raise funds for my travel costs. Soon, Greg Davis, Jon Edwards, and Grant organized parties in Bethesda, Georgetown, and Philadelphia. Caitlin and I attended each of these gatherings with deep gratitude, both for the funds that were raised on my behalf and for the time they gave us to be with each other and with friends.

At the party in Philadelphia, I got an additional special surprise that entertained us all and lifted my spirits to a new high. Through friends of friends, Grant and one of my favorite medical school professors, Dr. Jon Morris, had contacted one of my heroes: Borat. Yes, the Sacha Baron Cohen character. I was—and am—obsessed with all things Borat. Baron Cohen had created him—and become famous in character—around the time that my mom passed away. Though nothing else could make me laugh or even smile then, Borat unlocked something in me, and I cried—out of laughter—the first time I watched him in action. I didn't bother to think too hard about why this loony character gave me that release. I took it for the blessing that it clearly was. What was important was that my torpor had finally met its kryptonite: a faux-Kazakhstani news reporter who interviews Americans to provide "cultural learnings of America for make benefit glorious nation of Kazakhstan." Absurd? Yes. Juvenile? Some would say so. I just appreciated that he provided me a respite from my struggles (and I think he's brilliant).

I became a superfan during college. I dressed up as Borat and faithfully stayed in character for Halloween five years in a row. Caitlin put up with it. I even turned to Borat for help when I struggled with dissecting a human cadaver in my medical school anatomy lab, speaking only in his Kazakh accent to my lab partners during hours-long dissections to ease some of the discomfort I felt cutting into another human. No one in my class was surprised when I dressed up as Borat for class one day and asked the professor a question in Borat's style and accent. "He [the obese, shirtless, hairy man photographed on the screen] remind me of my wife, but my wife much more hairy than him. Does she have his condition?"

But then there in Houston Hall at the University of Pennsylvania, Borat was talking to me. Sacha Baron Cohen had filmed a video message for me while on the set of one of his movies. He called me the wrong name twice (intentionally) and also said that he could understand exactly what I was going through because he had gone through an entire box of tissues the previous week for a really, really bad cold. He ended by thanking the organizers for raising the funds for the event, which, he said, would actually all be used to pay for his special video appearance. I was touched by the huge effort that Grant and Dr. Morris had gone to to get Borat to talk to me on camera. I was beyond buoyed by his message.

I sent a glowing thank-you email replete with photo attachments of me dressed in character to Sacha Baron Cohen's agent. It was a long email. I had a lot to say. I probably shouldn't have been surprised when he sent a reply through his agent with the subject line "remove my email address." I guess he could sense I had some obsessive tendencies and didn't want me to even think about being able to email him on demand.

Being a patient with a rare disease—one I hoped would stay

in remission—gave me another area to put my *think it, do it* motto into practice.

I had seen firsthand how scarce research dollars and attention get funneled toward common diseases since the "upside"—the number of patients who might benefit (and subsequently pay for a potential new treatment)—is proportionately larger. This was a long-standing and, from the outside, not totally irrational concept. But the less common diseases often have more to be learned, more "low-hanging fruit," and far fewer existing solutions, so small research investments can go a long way for them and potentially have an even greater impact on patient lives.

I understood that I was unlikely to change the amount of research funding being distributed—diseases that affect larger populations are probably always going to get the biggest dollars—but it seemed to me that the system for awarding research dollars was not as streamlined and logical as it might be. I started to see that a more deliberate process might lead to less sporadic breakthroughs for diseases small and large. I was eager to dig into these big problems and work toward systemic solutions.

Just as I was getting interested in these problems, and soon after I returned to campus, a large anonymous donation was made to establish the Orphan Disease Center at the University of Pennsylvania. *Orphan* here is used to describe rare diseases, because they are often so neglected. It was serendipity, truly. The former dean of the University of Pennsylvania medical school, Dr. Arthur Rubenstein, was named interim director of the center. I had never met him but had heard him lecture and knew him to be a legend in endocrinology research and treatment and in academic medical leadership.

I emailed Dr. Rubenstein to offer to assist with the center in any way that I could. I may not have had an MD degree yet or the most impressive CV, but I thought that my personal battle with an orphan disease would be important. I was also on an experimental orphan disease drug. And founding AMF had given me experience building and growing an organization. I highlighted each of these points in my lengthy email and pressed send. I knew that the chances of a meeting with Dr. Rubenstein were slim to none—at least not for months; he was a very busy and sought-after man—but I found a friend in his assistant, Fran, who put me into his schedule when he had a cancellation just a few days later. A tight deadline is a gift for someone who likes to hyperfocus. In advance of the meeting, I spent dozens of hours putting together a detailed document describing the challenges in rare disease research and what I thought the center could accomplish. When we met, Dr. Rubenstein—whom I was now encouraged to call Arthur—saw how passionate I was. I couldn't have hidden it if I tried. He invited me to join the search committee for a permanent director and shortly thereafter to spearhead the formulation of a strategic growth and operational plan for the center.

Arthur Rubenstein opened my eyes to—and continues to teach me—a new paradigm of leadership. Up until then, my sense of leadership was informed by football and by my own hard-charging style. Leading the conditioning line, pulling aside teammates who needed encouragement, playing through injuries. I had also seen leaders who motivated through fear, which was more common than you'd like to think in medicine. But not Arthur. He is soft-spoken, single-mindedly focused on doing what is morally right above all else, and dedicated to bringing out the best in people. He works relentlessly hard when he believes in something. In truth, he reminded me a great deal of my mother. He was exquisitely talented at delegating, inspiring, and focusing us on the center's mission: to save rare disease patients' lives.

He didn't care about rank or status. All ideas were equal. Even I, a lowly medical student, was encouraged to contribute my ideas. Executive assistants and administrators who hadn't worked with him before were surprised when he asked for their input during meetings. He never made anyone feel that he had more skills than they did. In fact, he emphasized the opposite: You *are* the experts. You know what is needed to accelerate rare disease research at Penn and beyond. His humble approach encouraged idea sharing and participation from everyone. It was eye-opening to see someone of his pedigree putting into practice something I was only just beginning to understand: Medicine wasn't just made up of the spear tip of doctors and nurses. It was a whole human enterprise, one that needed as much leadership as it did raw ingenuity. Medicine suffered when it was only the sum of its most technical and esoteric knowledge. It thrived when it was a team effort.

I was so grateful to be on that team and enthusiastically delivered on Arthur's request for me to lead the creation of the center's strategic plan. In so doing, I learned that though each particular disease might be rare, the collective numbers are astounding: There are approximately seven thousand rare diseases and 350 million people afflicted by them worldwide. One in ten Americans has a rare disease; half of these are children, and about 30 percent of these children will die before their fifth birthday. Approximately 95 percent of rare diseases do not have a single FDA-approved therapy because they are so poorly understood. Simply put, you can't create a targeted treatment when you don't know what needs to be targeted.

A popular misconception is that rare diseases are highly complex or resistant to scrutiny, that they're the mastermind supervillains of biology. More often than not their underlying pathologies are simpler than those of many common diseases and often involve a single genetic defect. And technologies now exist to identify targets for treatments and drugs that effectively modulate them to interrupt disease.

Cystic fibrosis is a good example of what can happen when research and biomedical capabilities are aligned. A deadly genetic disease that causes persistent lung infections and limits the ability to breathe in approximately 30,000 Americans (which qualifies it as "rare" or "orphan" because it affects fewer than 200,000), cystic fibrosis has continually become more manageable with the development of new, life-extending drugs. This didn't happen by chance: It's a matter of numbers, coordination, and willpower of key individuals. The patient community has raised hundreds of millions of dollars for research. The leading foundation, the Cystic Fibrosis Foundation, has worked relentlessly to align all stakeholders. And biomedical research titans like Dr. Francis Collins, who is the current director of the National Institutes of Health, performed seminal research that propelled the field forward. Unfortunately, this is an exception. Even when there's a will, the lack of coordination, organization, and financing often slows things down. Approximately 50 percent of all rare diseases lack a disease-specific foundation to steward research; still others with foundations could stand to improve coordination of research studies, data, and biospecimens as well as collaboration between players.

The limited funding available for rare diseases magnifies the problem of inadequate coordination and collaboration across biomedical research and pushes researchers to work more independently and competitively rather than cooperatively. Some researchers fight to keep their patient biospecimens stored away rather than sharing with other researchers. Furthermore, the limited amount of data to build upon and systemic hurdles make it difficult to generate sufficient data to win federal funding. Federal funding agencies want to see a certain amount of preliminary data to award funding, but grant funding is needed to generate the level of data required for these agencies to award funding. It's a difficult cycle to break.

Of course, physicians can and do sometimes try "off-label" uses of treatments developed and approved for more common diseases to help rare disease patients when no FDA-approved treatments exist. Indeed doctors can prescribe just about any

FDA-approved drug to any patient for any medical condition at any time, whether it is approved by the FDA for that particular disease or not (whether an insurance company will pay for this use is another issue!). After all, many diseases share dysfunctional genes, proteins, or cells, which theoretically could be targeted with a common treatment. And sometimes targeting multiple diseases with the same treatment pays off: Viagra has been used successfully for pulmonary hypertension, Botox for unrelenting headaches, and the blood pressure medication propranolol for the deadly cancer angiosarcoma.

But here again there are big systemic barriers that stand in the way of using off-label drugs to advance science and patient care: The uses and effectiveness of these treatments are rarely tracked or aggregated, so future physicians are not able to build upon the results of previous treatment attempts to make future care decisions. Thus, some patients are started on a treatment that had never worked before while other patients are never started on an off-label treatment that is almost guaranteed to work, because of a lack of data. This is particularly painful and paradoxical in a time when so much data are being generated. The more I looked into the realities behind some rare diseases, the more the situation seemed to resemble the dysfunctional organization of intelligence and police forces before 9/11—everyone was doing their best job individually, but no one talked to one another, no prime database existed, there was no expectation of coordination or data sharing.

My crash course on the world of orphan diseases did reveal some bright spots and brilliant leaders. One such leader was Dr. Dan Rader, a distinguished physician-scientist at the University of Pennsylvania whom I first met through the Orphan Disease Center. He had recently conducted research that suggested that a drug sitting on a shelf at a major pharmaceutical company might be effective for patients with a deadly genetic disease called homozygous familial hypercholesterolemia. It was not being used because the side effect profile was too severe to try it in the general population. But the genetic condition was causing children and adolescents to die, and Dan thought this drug might work for them. He knew his patients (and their parents) would be willing to deal with the side effects if the drug could extend their lives. Dan worked with the drug company to study its efficacy. Sure enough, the trial was successful and resulted in an FDA approval. A drug sitting on the sidelines, waiting to save lives, had been neglected until the right person asked the right questions. How many more of these drugs were out there waiting to be deployed for the right disease?

Was there one for Castleman disease?

And how many drugs are already FDA-approved to treat one disease that are also effective at treating another disease and possibly many more? This was a line of questioning that I would never again put down. I became consumed with the idea that many of the answers we sought were already available. They'd just been forgotten, ignored, or not yet connected to the right questions. Kind of like a game of *Jeopardy!* but with really high stakes.

The bottom line I took from my work with Arthur and the Orphan Disease Center team was that organization mattered. I'd seen dysfunctional teams before. I'd even contributed to some. But I also knew what a singularly focused leader could do, as a point of connection around which a team can unite. I was never the fastest runner or farthest thrower, but I was a good quarterback. Each rare disease needs one.

Another rare disease quarterback that I met around this time was Josh Sommer. He had dropped out of Duke a few years before when he was diagnosed with chordoma—a rare bone cancer that often appears in the skull and spine—to create the Chordoma Foundation. He didn't create just any old foundation that directs funds for research. He created a force for change, invested in the creation of publicly available resources, and connected researchers around the world. His leadership has led to research breakthroughs and multiple promising clinical trials. As I listened to his story in a crowded and noisy coffee shop, I thought: *Should I be doing this for Castleman disease?*

Then, Josh interrupted my thoughts: "David," he said, "you're uniquely qualified to make an impact. It may not be my place to say this, but Castleman disease needs you."

I spent the next few days convincing myself that my time and energy should be focused on growing AMF and becoming an oncologist. I felt sure that others were on the case: Castleman disease already had two dedicated foundations, the International Castleman Disease Organization and Castleman's Awareness & Research Effort. I assumed they were both pushing research forward as quickly as possible. I decided to remain on the sidelines, hoping and praying that some researcher somewhere would figure out my disease. But a seed of an idea had been planted.

Medical school meant more clinical rotations. Pediatrics. Internal medicine. Family medicine. Interventional radiology. Emergency medicine. Rheumatology. On each rotation, I saw doctors and residents daily who had treated me when I was so sick. I didn't remember most of them, but they remembered me. Every time I'd pass them, they'd say, "David, you look so great!" I think this was quite confusing to the other physicians I was working with, who had no idea I was ever sick. "You look great" isn't typically how physicians greet one another in the hospital.

My free time during the week was spent working on the Orphan Disease Center and the weekends with Caitlin. I let myself believe that I was healthy. That the previous months of hell had been a deviation from what would be my normal, contented life.

Though I stayed away from conducting Castleman disease

research, I did end up writing a case report on a Castleman disease patient (me). I wanted to highlight how the eruption of those blood moles or cherry hemangiomas could be a sign that someone may have iMCD or will soon have a relapse, which had happened to me each time. The journal *JAMA Dermatology* published the case report and put a photograph of the blood moles on my bare chest on the cover. That was a first—I was a cover model!

I hoped that awareness of these blood moles would help to diagnose other patients more quickly, detect relapses earlier, and serve as a piece for solving the puzzle of this mysterious disease. And I secretly hoped the doctors who had scolded me to "forget the blood moles" would receive copies.

I was thinking and then doing.

And I was beginning to breathe easy.

CHAPTER TWELVE

But I already had a second Red Bull today.
And I got enough sleep last night.
I have too much to do.
Why am I so tired?
Why?

I was on a rotation in Pennsylvania Hospital when it started again in April 2012. I was listening to a patient tell me how he was feeling after knee surgery when suddenly the fatigue that I'd been fighting all day crystallized into a familiar feeling. I watched the man's lips move. The sounds from the room faded away. So much was going through my head. I excused myself and rushed to a room where I often studied between seeing patients. It was a part of the original hospital. During peaceful moments in the past, I'd imagined that Ben Franklin, who'd founded the hospital back in 1751, could have been in this same room many times.

Maybe he'd come here for some privacy, just as I did. Taken off his wig and kicked back.

But medical history wasn't on my mind today. I needed a nap, and I needed to tamp down my mounting anxiety. I shut the door, balled up my white coat into a makeshift pillow, set my alarm for seven minutes later, and lay down on the floor. Just as I closed my eyes, I calmed myself with a reminder: *You're getting siltuximab every three weeks. It's the drug. It targets the problem in this disease. There's no way you're relapsing. You're just tired. You're just tired.*

That night, I literally and figuratively sat on my hands and considered whether I should feel my neck for enlarged lymph nodes. This line of thought was totally irrational—I didn't have anything at all to gain by not knowing, and reaching up to palpate my own neck was something I wouldn't be able to avoid long term. But I knew mine was a common enough attitude. Every doctor has encountered patients who waited too long, even when they suspected that something was wrong, to seek help. They didn't want to know. I'd often been frustrated with these people. Now I understood.

Needing to know won out, and I found exactly what I didn't want to. Bulges along both sides of my neck. *But a lot of things can cause enlarged lymph nodes,* I thought. Which was true. True enough to warrant inaction for the night.

The next morning, however, I emailed my doctors to confess that I had not done the PET/CT scan they had recommended I do in January, a test that would detect new disease activity. I explained that with all of my responsibilities for the Orphan Disease Center and medical school rotations, I hadn't wanted to give up an entire morning to the scan process. But now—three months after I should have had the follow-up scan, which could have detected early signs of disease activity—I had new symptoms. I was told to get to the scanner the very next day.

When I spoke to Caitlin that night, I told her about my day and we planned our next visit. But I didn't mention the new symptoms. I didn't want her to worry. It was probably nothing. I was holding back on the transparency and vulnerability I had committed to give her, but, I reasoned, no one wants to hear about every ache and pain, and until I knew that this wasn't just a cold or the flu, she didn't need to go down the rabbit hole of worry with me. With the benefit of hindsight, I can see now: I was *that* afraid.

That night I woke up in a cold sweat; the sheets were completely soaked. When I got up to change them, I saw the last piece of evidence I needed: The blood moles were back, all over my torso.

I permitted myself one more cycle of magical thinking: I couldn't be relapsing, because I was taking siltuximab. Siltuximab would prevent relapses, as Dr. van Rhee had said. Full stop. I was healthy.

Everything was fine. It had to be. I *knew* that my disease couldn't come back while I was on this experimental drug. I'd gotten my miracle. The kind of miracle my mother hadn't had for her cancer, and so many others don't get for their diseases either. If siltuximab actually couldn't stop my disease or prevent relapses . . .

My patient-self retreated somewhere dark. My diagnostician-self took the tiller.

I pulled up my PET/CT results on my phone the next day as I walked to a patient's room. The scan indicated that my lymph nodes were as large as they had been when I was hospitalized the first time around *and* they had increased metabolic activity. This should have indicated a relapse and prompted immediate blood work and a dose of siltuximab. I would have recommended exactly that course had I been my own patient. But I was still my old, stubborn self: I explained to my doctors that I needed to complete the clinical rotation I was on, and

besides, I had a lot to do to prepare for AMF's annual fundraising gala, which was on Friday in Raleigh. And actually, then we
had an important AMF board meeting on Monday, so the blood
work and dose of siltuximab would have to occur on Tuesday.
And I then explained it the same way to Caitlin. I downplayed
the significance of the needed blood work to her just as much as
I did to myself. She was concerned but comforted by the expla-
nations—or rationalizations—that I had for everything that was
happening.

Don't worry, I thought and said. *It can't be a relapse.*

Unfortunately, my doctors trusted my judgment, and I didn't
get blood work until a week after I'd felt my enlarged lymph
nodes. Several test results were abnormal. The most important
one we were monitoring was C-reactive protein (CRP), a
marker of inflammation and immune system activation. During
my three previous flare-ups, it was my most reliable disease
marker, spiking when I worsened, rising above 300 at my sickest, and improving when I felt better. It was *the* test, and it had
remained normal for the last year.

The number did come back elevated, but only slightly, to
12.7. The normal range was 0 to 10. What's 2.7 points above
normal when you've touched 300? It was an enormous relief. I
got back to thinking that I was overreacting, that I was only
feeling a little sick with a garden-variety virus, just like anyone
else. After all, I'd had a sore throat. Maybe the sore throat could
explain why my CRP was mildly elevated? Based on my enlarged and newly active lymph nodes, my doctors decided to
administer a dose of siltuximab a week earlier than the usual
spacing. Just to be safe.

As during all of my previous infusions, my sister Gena sat
next to me and I worked on my computer with complete focus
on whatever AMF emails or Orphan Disease Center documents
I was working on. *Today is just like any other day,* I kept telling

myself. I decided to stay in Raleigh and repeat blood work in two days. Just to be safe.

Two days later, my CRP had shot up to 227. This was shocking above and beyond its indication that I was truly relapsing; a spike from 12.7 to 227 so quickly was almost unthinkable. So my doctor and I did what every good practitioner should when he or she gets a weird number: recheck the result.

It appeared correct—until we looked back at the previous report and realized that the CRP level was measured in different units at the different hospitals. The 12.7 reading was a measurement in milligrams per deciliter, not milligrams per liter, as we were used to. That meant that our decimal point was in the wrong spot. Tuesday's CRP level had actually been 127.

We should have already been panicking.

Not only was my iMCD coming back, but its intensity had doubled in just two days, even *after* I'd been given the drug that was supposed to treat it. It felt like Castleman disease was taunting me, toying with me, showing just how much more powerful it was than the treatment into which I had channeled all of my hope.

Since our new weapon had failed, my doctors reverted to an old trick: I was immediately given a dose of the chemotherapy that had worked for my second flare (even though it didn't work for my third one). We were now fully grasping at straws.

I gathered myself, and I called Caitlin. No more rationalizing what was happening. It's not some strange cold. It's back, I admitted. I knew that she had decided to be with me fully cognizant that I still had the disease in me and that it could come back at any time, but I couldn't *not* feel like this was somehow a betrayal. I hated that I had to "test" her so quickly. I hated that she had to think of these things at all. She was still living in New York, but she made arrangements to meet me in Philadelphia before my father and I would fly to Little Rock; she would come to Arkansas a bit later with my sisters. This would be her first time seeing me battle iMCD. She couldn't get into Philadelphia until that evening, so I went to see each of my closest med school friends over the course of the day. This routine of saying goodbye was something I'd done before.

By the time Caitlin arrived, I'd pulled myself together and was projecting positivity. It was true that I was relapsing yet again, but there was something almost comforting in the serial nature of my disease course: I'd gotten sick three times before, yes, but I also hadn't died three times! I had an amazing doctor, who was very good at keeping me alive. And he must have tons of new tricks up his sleeve after the last year of work by Santa's helpers.

It had been fifteen months since I was in this hospital. Not much had changed in Little Rock, at least at the hospital. It was still the center of the Castleman disease world, still bursting with hope in various forms. Overeager smiles, firm handshakes, clipped green lawns, and that same brick-and-glass hospital architecture that connoted quick, semihurried service the world over.

I was different, though. I had the collective wisdom of the past year plus in my pocket. I had the private potency of *think it, do it* in mind. I had gotten plenty of chemotherapy in the past. I felt like I could handle anything.

I was also overconfident. The results of new blood tests in Little Rock came back far worse than they had been in Raleigh. Castleman disease was back and it was roaring. Within a couple days of arriving at UAMS, my liver, kidneys, bone marrow, heart, and lung functions were all deteriorating. I'd seen these lab abnormalities before in myself and my patients. I'd dealt with bad results and bad news. But never had a series of lab tests brought so much disappointment and such a definitive implication. I kept returning to the horrible disappointment that all this was happening while I was on treatment with siltuximab.

My relapse meant one of two things:

1. I actually somehow *hadn't* received siltuximab due to a mistake, or I had received the wrong dose of siltuximab. (I rated this unlikely.)
2. The only drug in development for my disease wasn't working, and I had no other options. This also would mean that the medical community was wrong: IL-6 was not the problem for all patients with iMCD, so siltuximab would not help everyone with my disease. (I rated this as likely.)

These two possibilities were quickly whittled down to one: Detailed hospital auditing records confirmed that I had received siltuximab at the appropriate dose for the previous fifteen months. Everything had gone as it should have, and I had gotten very sick anyway.

We were back to square one. The only thing the medical community "knew" about iMCD was not correct for me. Interleukin 6 was not the problem for everyone with iMCD. Siltuximab wouldn't work for everyone, including me.

The siltuximab that I had been on for the previous year and the single dose of chemotherapy I had received a few days before in Raleigh were clearly not slowing things down, so Dr. van Rhee decided to take the "shock and awe" approach again. I was immediately started on the same combination of seven chemotherapies as before. Like before, the cocktail targeted my immune cells and other rapidly dividing cells like my bone marrow, hair, and intestines.

I needed answers. I may or may not have been approaching death for the *fourth* time. As the chemo cocktail dripped into my arm through the IV pole at my side, I asked Dr. van Rhee everything I had been obsessing over since I started to feel sick again.

"What causes this to happen?"

"No one knows."

"Which type of immune cell is responsible for initiating this?"

"No one knows."

Why not? I wanted to ask.

And why me?

I swallowed those final questions, but a hospital room is never, ever silent, even in the dead of night, or even when a conversation grinds to a halt and the participants are left to quietly pick at the implications of what's been said, and what's been impossible to say.

It occurred to me, between the periodic beeps from my IV pole, that Dr. van Rhee was not saying "I don't know" to my queries about my illness. He might have said "I'm not sure, let me look that up . . ." and swiveled over to his computer to plug in the symptoms and dial up some answers. But he didn't say that. He said "No one knows."

"Are there any other drugs in development or clinical trials?"

Dr. van Rhee was unfailingly calm and caring when he responded to my most important question. "No, not at the moment."

"Are there any planned?"

"Not that I'm aware of."

Dr. van Rhee was the undisputed worldwide expert on Castleman disease, and he didn't know what initiated the disease or what caused it. Or how to prevent relapses in patients for whom the only experimental treatment in development didn't work. That meant that *no* one knew. There were no more appeals. There was no higher bench. He was not flattering himself by speaking on behalf of the world's knowledge of my condition. He *was* that knowledge. He didn't just have authority; he *was* the authority.

As a medical student, I could select the correct answer to each of these questions for what seemed like every disease, but not this one.

"I know elevated interleukin 6 is supposed to be the problem, but blocking it hasn't worked twice now and my interleukin 6 tests were normal during my presentation and relapses. Is it possible that interleukin 6 isn't the problem for all cases?"

"It's possible."

That was it. It was possible. *Anything* was possible.

I knew what he meant. I knew the language that doctors use: the careful truth telling, the hedging, the open-endedness. I'd spoken that language before. Now that it was directed at me, it didn't feel nearly as careful, or open-ended, as I'd once assumed. Instead, the words felt like they were casting me out of the room, out of the hospital entirely. I'd been consigned to the plane of *possibility*. Anything was possible, because no one knew. I was on my own.

A proper patient might have taken Dr. van Rhee's pronouncements with humility and acceptance, but *no one knows* didn't cut it for me. There are things we can change and things we cannot change. We need either the grace to accept them, the ignorance to not know the difference, or prayers to find another expert who has the answers. I am not graceful. I was no longer ignorant of the realities of iMCD. And I was getting tired of praying.

A whole mental structure built on faith and expectation—or hubris—collapsed for me that day. When Dr. van Rhee entered that room to discuss my disease rationally—doctor to emerging doctor—I had believed there had been a vast, unseen, but highly coordinated system of scientists, companies, and physicians working diligently to cure my disease. Every disease, actually. Of course there was—right?

Like Santa and his elves working to grant wishes to every good boy and girl in the world, I imagined that for every problem in the world, a highly qualified team worked diligently, perhaps in a workshop, and it operated out of sight, out of mind, right up until the moment that it solved the problem. Right on schedule, deposited in your living room, and wrapped in a bow, the problem is solved, revealing the magic of the workshop's efforts. Google reinforces this belief. For every question you can think of, Google provides an answer—and often data to back it up—with a speed and precision that inspire confidence, if not always comfort. The frequent news about medical breakthroughs feeds this optimistic illusion: You assume that someone, somewhere has already figured out the answer to every medical question you could ever pose or, if not, that a team is hard at work solving your particular puzzle, to meet your particular medical need as quickly as possible. A cure is near; discoveries will happen whether or not you contribute time, talent, or dollars toward them. So, I had waited on the sidelines because I believed others were on the case. But now that illusion was no longer possible to sustain. Not when Santa Claus himself was looking me in the eyes and telling me nothing would materialize, giftwrapped, to cure me.

Nausea overwhelmed me, partly because of the chemotherapy cocktail that had been slowly dripping into my veins during our conversation, and partly because of the realization that I was completely alone. I was terrified. This was the fourth time in the last two years that I would approach the precipice of death. This time, I *knew* that I would die, because the only drug in development for my disease had failed to work. The harsh reality was that the medical community didn't understand the most basic aspects of my illness—the only thing the medical community "knew" to be true was actually wrong—and the world's expert in it had run out of ideas and options for me.

Despite the fact that my immune system was consuming all of my energy as it attacked my organs, despite the accumulated toxins and chemotherapy that made my thinking cloudy, I had the most clear and important thought of my young life: I could no longer just hope that my treatment would work. I could no longer rely on the previous research. I could no longer hope someone else, somewhere would perform research that would lead to breakthroughs that could save my life. If I were to survive again—and to survive long term—I had to get off the sidelines and act. If I didn't start fighting back to cure this disease, no one else would and I would soon die. I would never get to marry Caitlin or have a family with her. Dr. van Rhee was the foremost expert in the world on Castleman disease—Santa himself—but the foremost expert in the world can only ever know as much as the accumulated knowledge in the world. If the answers have not yet been uncovered, then the foremost expert couldn't possibly know them. These answers weren't Googleable, and prayers couldn't help to find the doctor who knew them. No one knew. Even worse, there were no promising leads being chased. The limits of Dr. van Rhee's potency were the limits of the world. They were also now my limits, and other patients' limits too.

My body was dying. I was in overtime. I was spent. But at least I wasn't on the sidelines anymore. Now I was in the game, and I knew what I had to do. I would simply have to increase the knowledge of the world about iMCD.

My sisters, Caitlin, and Dad were seated around the bed and had listened to Dr. van Rhee's every word. They all had their hands on their heads and stared down at the floor between long blinks and deep breaths.

I interrupted the silence by saying something that I hadn't ever voiced before but knew was my only choice. In hindsight, it reminds me of the final promise I made to my mom. "If I survive this, I'm going to dedicate the rest of my life—however long that may be—to answering these unknowns and curing this disease."

I heard myself like I was Winston Churchill vowing to fight on the beaches, but my pledge to defeat Castleman disease was less than stirring to Caitlin and my family. Those words in the hospital room landed with a polite thud. They each gave a half smile—a kind of smile that I had seen before. The one where they purse their lips and close their eyes. They were just focused on me making it through this relapse. They weren't interested in heroics. They too knew that we were in yet another overtime, and that the future no longer pertained.

I couldn't blame them. My family had watched this monster of a disease take me to the brink of death three times. They had also lost some of their optimism eight years before, when our mom's brain cancer relapsed after one year of treatment on the only promising drug at the time. With no other options, she died a few months later. Here I was, fifteen months after last being ravaged by my disease, and the only promising drug was not working. This was a situation familiar to everyone in that room.

But this was the moment when I realized that I was finally done with the passive kind of hope, the hope that waits for Santa Claus and gets in the way of action. To be sure, passive hope had helped me through multiple relapses. I don't think I would have survived the third one had I not met the patient in Dr. van Rhee's clinic who looked so healthy; his example sustained me.

But here, at last, I understood that hope on its own is often not enough. In my case, hope that my treatment would work and hope that some researchers somewhere would unravel iMCD impeded my taking action. And why not me? Suddenly, I saw that the road to what I was hoping for may be long, and I knew it was likely that I would never get to the hoped-for end. But I needed to start trekking.

Now I had to figure out what actions to take. And, of course, I had no guarantees that I would figure anything out or that my final days would not be spent working in vain to answer the unknowns of Castleman disease. In fact, I expected that my time would probably run out before I could make a meaningful impact for myself and other patients, but I wanted to go out swinging; there was no way to know unless I tried. I would make every second count, and my fourth overtime would be bigger than just me fighting to survive—it would be me fighting to extend survival for the thousands of other patients with my disease.

Soon, I began to feel the power of a closed circuit of hope and action: The more I imagined a long future with Caitlin and the possibility of children, the more the stultifying effects of fear and doubt dissipated. Then, action that led to meaningful progress inspired further hope for my future. The more I thought about the thousands of other patients with my disease and the many more who would be diagnosed in the future, the more I was inspired to act. Hope was the essential condition and fuel for my taking action at this point in my life. Fear disintegrates. Doubt disorganizes. Hope clears the way, pushes out the horizons, and gives us space to build structures. My hope was inaugurated by the strength that my family gave me, that Caitlin gave me, and, crucially, that I grabbed by the neck when I knew no one else would and decided to *take* it. *Think it, do it* is how I "programmatized" hope, how I turned it into action that I could take and make every day. Hope wasn't something precious I had to preserve; it was something strong, stronger than I was, that I hitched on to for dear life.

For years, I had interpreted the Pope John Paul II quote I'd found in my mother's purse—his call to be "invincible in hope"—as referring to being invincible *because* you can have faith that your hopes and prayers will come true. You just need to trust and wait. I'd read that line as meaning that taking action was almost in opposition to being invincible in hope. But I later found the remainder of the pope's speech. He went on to say:

> Happiness is achieved through sacrifice. Do not look outside for what is to be found inside. Do not expect from others what you yourselves can and are called to be or to do.

I became invincible in hope only after I realized I was called to act on—and with, and through—that hope. I knew what I needed to do.

But first things first: I asked the nurse for a dose of Zofran for my nausea. It's a lot harder to solve the thing that's killing you when you want to throw up. Especially when you're just a lowly medical student. Then I asked Gena if she could get a copy of my blood work. She wiped away her tears and sprang into action, eager to do something, anything that could help her little brother. I needed my test results so I could start studying my disease and also so I could estimate how much time I likely had before I'd be incapacitated by kidney and liver failure—or dead.

Then, I started squaring up to this beast of a disease. With three more days of continuous cytotoxic chemotherapy and then seventeen days of interspersed chemo ahead of me, my hair would soon start falling out in clumps, the way it had before. But I didn't want to wait for it to fall out again, and I didn't want this disease or chemotherapy to be the cause for it coming off. I was done being a victim. This time I would act: I asked my dad to buy an electric razor, and he shaved all my hair off, save a small strip of short hair down the middle. I had always wanted a Mohawk. I probably also should have covered my face in camo war paint. I was gearing up for a new kind of battle, one that wasn't simply about my surviving Castleman disease's attack—it would involve me counterattacking. And I was reminded of that every time I saw my high-and-tight look in the mirror.

CHAPTER THIRTEEN

AS THE BIG day approached, I got more and more nervous.

Dr. van Rhee was concerned that I might not be healthy enough and my immune system not strong enough. My dad echoed his concerns, saying I needed more time before I made such a hasty decision. Knowing how disappointed I would be, Dr. van Rhee brought my favorite Trini dish to the hospital that night. It *was* a great consolation.

But I knew what I needed to do. I knew what I had promised.

Finally, with just days to spare, Dr. van Rhee came back with the results and told me that my white blood cells had reached the threshold we had discussed. It was time.

I left the hospital, got on a plane, and returned to Raleigh.

I wasn't going to miss Ben's wedding.

The carpet bombing worked. I recovered again. Don't ask me how. I don't know. I'd gone through hell again, and I came back. We didn't know what treatment to try next, but that didn't matter as I stood as Ben's best man at the altar looking out at a congregation that included my father, my sisters, and the love of my life, Caitlin. Pictures of that day show my freshly bald head— not from the chemo, but because *I* shaved it—and a smile from ear to ear. I almost look deranged. I'm smiling because I'm upright and (mostly) feeling fine, and because I'm there with everyone I love. And because I'm fulfilling one of my promises to Ben from high school that I never thought I was going to be able to keep.

But I'm also smiling for another reason.

With football, I think I may have gotten more sheer pleasure out of preparing for than actually playing the game. The film study, the lifting, the drills, the practice, the meetings, the strategy. It was the same with AMF: I loved whiteboarding in the AMF office about how to expand our reach or improve our services. And in school I'd taken strange (certainly to my friends) satisfaction in sitting at a long table in the library, books ready, pencil in hand, papers meticulously placed across the table, perched on the edge of a marathon study session.

That smile at the wedding? It's the smile of a man who knows what he's about to do. It's the smile before the storm. After round four, all my thinking had been done, now it was time for the doing. I felt like Jason Bourne in the fourth act: battered, bloody, totally broken down—but with a plan. No one more dangerous than someone with nothing to lose and a head full of steam.

The hyperfocus helps too.

After a few weeks recovering in North Carolina, I returned to medical school. I would continue to receive siltuximab and weekly doses of three of the seven chemotherapies that had just induced my remission. We reasoned that maybe siltuximab in combination with these other drugs would work even if it hadn't worked on its own. And even if my IL-6 levels had been normal previously. I didn't feel very confident that this approach would work long term, but I just didn't have any other options.

As I look back, I see that everything that had happened in my life had prepared me for this. I didn't have the specific experiences to pursue a cure for a disease, but I had the tools. I had the work ethic that bordered on obsession. I had the institutional memory of building AMF, which provided me with a blueprint and confidence knowing I could execute. I would lean on lessons learned from my years as a quarterback to build and develop a team. My master's at Oxford gave me a framework for studying and answering highly complex questions. My nearly complete medical school coursework and clinical rotations gave me the language, understanding of disease mechanisms, and training that I'd need. What I learned from performing strategic planning for the Penn Orphan Disease Center informed the approach that I'd take. Losing Caitlin when I thought we had all the time in the world and never wanting to lose her again gave me an unrelenting sense of urgency and helped me to prioritize the most important things in life. And, significantly, I had finally internalized the idea that sharing my vulnerabilities would be a good thing and even important for mobilizing others to help. Caitlin and my family gave me all the love and support I would desperately need.

To take on Castleman disease, I would first need to understand the current state of research: what was known about the disease, what research was being done, and what steps other rare disease groups had taken to advance research for their diseases. I was like a detective who arrives at the murder scene and quickly gathers info from the cops already there. No one had solved the crime yet, but their legwork would be crucial to getting a lead.

Though Castleman disease was discovered in 1954, the only real advance in understanding my subtype had been in pinpointing IL-6 as a likely actor underlying the disease. But for me, IL-6 had not yet proven to be the main issue, so for me, the only real advance since 1954 was a misstep. Inaccurate information about epidemiology and prognosis was on reputable medical resources, including the UpToDate page that I now knew to be ironically and woefully out of date. Other websites weren't just out of date, they were objectively wrong. There was not a unique International Classification of Diseases (ICD) code to identify and track cases of Castleman disease—so even when doctors diagnosed Castleman disease patients, there was no way to identify them for future research and for the wider medical community to better understand. Many researchers and physicians were using different terminologies to subclassify Castleman disease, and still others lumped all Castleman disease cases together, so readers of published research articles wouldn't know which subtype the paper was referring to or be able to understand the results in the context of previous research. In short, the state of Castleman disease affairs was a mess.

Messes are worse in science than anywhere else, because science is quintessentially iterative. Everything builds on the past, on the last experiment, on the last theory, on the last results. Common standards of terminology and measurement are the sine qua non of the whole shebang. Basically, you need to be sure everyone is separating the apples from the oranges in a consistent way.

What I quickly found was that my particular subtype of Castleman disease, iMCD, which we now knew accounted for about 50 percent of MCD cases, totaling about one thousand new diagnoses each year in the United States, received little attention or funding compared to even the other subtypes of MCD. In fact, iMCD had received zero dollars in federal funding for research and treatment discovery. And since it occupied a no-man's-land between autoimmune diseases and cancers, no one knew which of the two categories to place it in. This meant that even private funding sources for cancer and autoimmune research wouldn't back it. It was the orphan of the orphans.

Unsurprisingly, no one knew the cause, the immune cell types, or the cellular communication lines involved in iMCD, impeding drug discovery.

The news got worse.

Major silos existed between physicians, researchers, and patients with iMCD. Dr. van Rhee had the only lab dedicated to studying iMCD, but there were also researchers in France, Japan, and a few other locations around the United States that would occasionally perform studies of iMCD along with related diseases. However, few of these disparate researchers had ever even met, and none had shared biospecimens or research ideas. This meant that case reports and studies with small patient numbers (therefore inadequately powered to generate meaningful conclusions) were the default. Most blood and tissue biospecimens collected from patients were discarded after testing was performed for patient care. Among the biospecimens that were kept for research, nearly all were sitting in lab freezers in separate locations around the world rather than being studied, let alone studied together. No registries or biobanks existed for storing data or biospecimens in a central place. No large-scale efforts had been made to systematically characterize the clinical and pathological abnormalities of iMCD, something that has been done for nearly all diseases. On top of that, research was completely uncoordinated. There was no agreed-upon framework for how the disease was believed to work to guide research or propose hypothesized mechanisms.

The only dedicated research effort going on at the time was the development of a so-called panoptic IL-6 blood test. A couple of recent studies had revealed that IL-6 levels were not coming back elevated in many iMCD patients, which led some to believe that the IL-6 tests being used must have been inaccurate. This theory concerned me: Trusting a result only when it's what you expect and then assuming the test is wrong when you get a result that you do not expect is antithetical to science. Even so, it would be important to determine if these normal IL-6 levels in iMCD patients were accurate. Of course, it could just be that IL-6 wasn't elevated in those patients and other factors were at play.

Nevertheless, a few treatments were being used with some anecdotal success, but there were no treatment guidelines and no databases or registries to systematically track and identify the most effective options. No wonder the Duke doctors didn't know what else to try after their first treatment didn't immediately work, and even Dr. van Rhee had a limited arsenal. Thanks to the groundbreaking discovery by Kazu Yoshizaki (remember the Japanese doctor who experimented on himself?) of elevated IL-6 in a couple Castleman disease patients in 1989, drugs targeting IL-6 (siltuximab) and the IL-6 receptor (tocilizumab) had been investigated in clinical trials for the treatment of iMCD. They worked in similar ways, so patients who didn't improve with one were unlikely to improve with the other. Unfortunately, there were no additional drugs or potential targets for treatment being studied other than IL-6 for patients who don't respond to these drugs.

It was now also clear why it had been so difficult to diagnose my case. There were no diagnostic criteria for any of the subtypes of Castleman disease. This meant that doctors didn't have a checklist of tests to run or results to expect to diagnose iMCD. Even worse, many other diseases—like lymphoma, lupus, and mononucleosis—can demonstrate similar signs and symptoms to iMCD. So patients had to just hope that their physicians even knew about iMCD to consider it, hope that their physicians were aware of some of the testing that could be done based on reading medical journal articles, and hope that their physicians knew what to look for in the test results to diagnose it. That's the wrong kind of hope. That would be like expecting a pilot to successfully fly a plane she had never flown before to a destination she had never traveled to without any map or any instructions. It's *possible* she'd figure out takeoff, navigation to the destination, and landing, but she would have no guidelines to increase her chances of getting there safely.

The more I learned, the more I realized how little the medical community knew about iMCD and how unlikely they were to make any meaningful progress in the near future on the current path. That was intellectually dispiriting—and personally devastating. Not only did Santa Claus not exist, but now it was as though the Santa Claus at the mall that you'd always looked up to was an evil, criminal mastermind. Just not existing would have been enough, thanks.

And a lack of progress wasn't for a lack of intelligence or the best of intentions among members of the community. Rather, it became clear to me that we were dealing with a problem of mission and organization. Though the two existing foundations, International Castleman Disease Organization and Castleman's Awareness & Research Effort, provided lifesaving referrals to a small group of experts and generated important awareness and research funding, neither foundation was playing the quarterback role that is so desperately needed for rare diseases—building the research community, consolidating their knowledge, identifying gaps in understanding, prioritizing the most likely fruitful research, forging collaborations between complementary partners, and ultimately propelling understanding toward a cure. We needed to coalesce into an army and charge forward with a unifying mission. I still believed that it was entirely possible the cure already existed, and just hadn't been properly marshaled. Perhaps its pieces existed, but in different labs in different parts of the world.

This effort to cure Castleman disease would be a challenge for a leader as much as for a researcher. I set out to become both. I decided that I wasn't going to reform any existing structures. Instead, I was going to build something new.

The first person I wanted to meet with to discuss my plans

to take on iMCD was Arthur Rubenstein. He told me I would have his full support, and he'd meet with me as often as was needed. He kept that promise. We'd end up meeting every couple of weeks for the next six years (and counting) to overcome scientific, organizational, and collaborative challenges. Arthur would lean on decades of experience navigating biomedical research and discovery to predict challenges before they arose and advise on preventive measures that we could take. And when unavoidable and seemingly insurmountable challenges did arise, we systematically worked toward solutions and frequently pulled in others for advice. I could never have predicted just how much of an impact Arthur would have, but he has been the most incredible mentor, colleague, and friend.

I knew from my work on AMF and from Arthur's sage advice that understanding the lay of the land—the present sad state of iMCD research coordination—was an essential first step. Now, I needed to understand what approaches and steps other disease fields had taken to overcome similar challenges (there are no points for originality in medicine).

What I discovered wasn't that much more heartening. Josh Sommer's work with the Chordoma Foundation was the exception, not the rule. Instead most rare disease research funding organizations raised money, invited researchers to submit research proposals describing how they would use the funds to answer an important research question, and then selected the best proposal for funding. It was random, uncoordinated, and reactive. They hoped that the right researcher with the right skill set and the right biospecimens would apply for funding to conduct the right project at the right time.

This model works well for the NIH and other large funding bodies, because they get thousands of applications from the best minds in the world, so the top proposed studies are likely to be some of the most important studies for their fields. But most rare diseases don't have NIH-funded investigators. Instead, foundations focused on a single rare disease may have to select from among only a handful of applicants. And when the number of interested and qualified researchers in an area is limited to just a few, it is unlikely that the applications will propose the most important studies and be submitted by the most qualified researchers. It wasn't a knock on those researchers; it was just a matter of numbers. This approach was like waiting for the stars to align. When you have tons and tons and tons of stars, they do align every once in a while. But when you have just a few, you'll be waiting for a long time. Too long, especially if you're a patient; it felt like a peacetime model with no urgency. And I was at war.

The other, knock-on effect of this small-pool competition was that each study was often conceived of and developed independently from the others, preventing a coordinated, disease-wide plan from emerging. It also meant that biospecimens and research ideas were often assets for researchers to list in grant applications to distinguish themselves from others rather than shared for collective discovery. If the given grant application wasn't funded, the biospecimens often remained untouched for the next application. Biospecimens filled with myriad insights to be uncovered often sat on the sidelines, no matter how promising other researchers' work was. This was just plain wasteful. Not because of anyone's bad intentions or laziness, but because the major scale model that worked for more common diseases just did not scale for "smaller" diseases. Common diseases don't necessarily require the same level of cross-institutional collaboration as rare diseases, because single institutions have large enough patient numbers to identify powerful patterns on their own. Not so for rare diseases. Patient samples are inherently scarce. No single researcher can do it alone. There has to be sample sharing to achieve the numbers needed to reach meaningful insights. We needed to rethink the whole operation, the whole field. We *didn't* need to build yet another silo.

I decided that I would take two paths forward: I would conduct laboratory and clinical research into iMCD during my last
year of medical school at the University of Pennsylvania and
cofound the Castleman Disease Collaborative Network (CDCN)
with Dr. van Rhee to accelerate research, diagnostics, and treatment discovery for Castleman disease internationally. Our goal
is to identify an effective treatment for every Castleman disease
patient. I realize this was quite ambitious. But I did have a secret
weapon helping me. Among the three weekly chemotherapies
that I was on, two of the drugs were supposed to wipe me out,
but one overcame the fatigue and even gave me seemingly endless energy. And a lot of impulsivity. This meant that for twenty-
four hours after my weekly chemotherapy day, I didn't sleep,
was hyperalert, and got tons of AMF and CDCN work done, if
hastily. Of course, being *able* to stay awake and alert for that long
was no guarantee that I was really operating effectively. As a
precaution, Caitlin read drafts of emails I wrote during those
bursts of productivity—we wanted to be sure that they weren't
too rambling, too erratic, or uncharacteristically candid.

When thinking about how the CDCN would accelerate research into how Castleman disease works and how to best diagnose and treat it, I came up with an ambitious but quite simple
plan (I thought!): Instead of waiting for the stars to align, we
would align the stars.

First, we'd need to identify, connect, and build a global community to identify and prioritize high-impact research projects.
Toward this end, we imagined an online crowdsourcing process
that allowed any patient, physician, or researcher to suggest lines
of inquiry or studies that seemed most important, regardless of
that person's ability to perform the study. This was a novel approach: The norm in medical research dictates that research ideas
are pursued if they're conceived by a researcher who can also
garner the necessary funding and do the work. Promising ideas,
if conceived by someone who can't obtain the funding or per-

form the work, go unharnessed. We couldn't afford to let that happen. We also proposed the creation of a scientific advisory board to prioritize the crowdsourced ideas based on their likely impact, feasibility, and rational order within an overarching framework (e.g., you shouldn't perform in-depth investigations of the inner workings of a particular cell type until after you have identified that the particular cell type is in fact important in Castleman disease). Once we had a list of priority studies, we'd recruit the best researchers in the world for those particular studies to conduct them. Of course and importantly, we'd need to reach out to patients and establish partnerships to gather samples and funding. Upon completion of every study, we would earmark time and resources to the search for medications already FDA-approved for other diseases that might be repurposed to target any of the discoveries made (e.g., cell types, molecules involved, etc.). And when medications were repurposed for use in iMCD, we'd systematically track their effectiveness to guide future use and identify promising candidates for clinical trials. Finally, we understood that feeding information back to the community would be the critical component to keep all of this going— sharing findings would promote continued rounds of crowdsourcing, prioritization, expert recruitment, and execution.

What we were proposing would maximize efficiency and give the best hope for breakthroughs in the shortest amount of time. Put simply, we'd bring all the key stakeholders together and then apply hyperfocus to research. Instead of soliciting grant applications and hoping that the right researcher would apply to conduct the right research, we'd ensure that the right research is done by the right researcher right now. It's the difference between a high school announcing that they're holding tryouts to fill the roster for a new football team and the focused and strategic work that the New England Patriots do to evaluate, identify, and recruit the best players in the world to their roster, who they also ensure will fit together as a team.

To build a community that could be crowdsourced to prioritize research, I needed to find everyone who had ever written a case report or scientific paper on Castleman disease in the last fifty years. In other words, I needed to search Google and PubMed, the NIH's repository of medical journal articles. A lot. There were about two thousand medical journal articles tagged with the term *Castleman disease*. I read every paper, extracted the key data for future analyses, and wrote to every author email address I could find. Each email was cosigned "David Fajgenbaum and Frits van Rhee." We worked really well together as cofounders, and it felt good to begin to transition into being colleagues instead of connected only through a patient-doctor relationship. I understood how ego-free he was to be willing to work alongside and mentor me, a patient and an aspiring doctor. The dual email signature also gave me some street cred when I was emailing physicians around the world: I was presenting myself as an interested medical student; I didn't feel comfortable sharing that I was also a patient. A few months and hundreds of emails later, we had connected a virtual community of about three hundred physicians and researchers around the world interested in Castleman disease through an online discussion board and invited them to attend an in-person meeting at the American Society of Hematology convention in December 2012 in Atlanta. ASH, as it's called in the field, is the largest hematology gathering in the world.

I couldn't sleep the night before the meeting. It wasn't because I had just gotten my oxymoronically energy-boosting chemo cocktail; I was excited and nervous. This meeting would help to establish what was currently known, put forth hypotheses for some of the gaps in knowledge, and the attendees would largely be our pool of potential CDCN scientific advisory board members.

Thirty-one physicians and researchers attended our meeting at the convention, which meant that it was the largest Castleman disease physician and researcher gathering ever, even larger than the only meeting ever held before, in 2005. And though it was no ESPY awards, for me it was just as exciting: I was starstruck meeting physicians whose names I recognized from my reading. Dr. Kazu Yoshizaki, the self-experimenter who had discovered the link between IL-6 and iMCD, was there with other colleagues from Japan. I even met Dr. Eric Oksenhendler, the lead author of the 1996 study listed on Wikipedia that had led me to tears when I saw the frighteningly low survival rates. I was also struck by the lack of consensus among the community and the paucity of research efforts.

A scientific advisory board was assembled soon after the meeting. In my excitement and eagerness for progress, I peppered each of these scientific and clinical heavyweights with endless questions. At least at the beginning—I clearly wore out my intellectual welcome with some of them. One board member gently took me aside and tried to explain that Castleman disease was no one physician's or researcher's priority and that I needed to lower my expectations for what everyone could contribute. After a talk I gave during a daylong research meeting at another institution some weeks later—where I was sternly instructed to share my patient experience only, but where I hijacked things and gave a presentation about the CDCN approach and research instead—I learned that some thought I was naïve to think that I or the CDCN could actually make a difference. They thought I was crossing into territory where I didn't belong. Many felt I should raise funds to support the existing research labs and stick to patient advocacy and awareness. A lab manager for one of those labs even *kindly* redid my PowerPoint slides before a meeting that showed the CDCN's multiple roles in connecting everyone. Her version had no network building. No research agenda setting. No collaborations. My relative youth and lack of formal hematology/oncology fellowship training were strikes against my mission it seemed, and the CDCN's unusual approach to research was deemed almost futile.

Had I not literally had skin in this game and a time bomb hidden beneath, I can't say that I wouldn't have once agreed with this emerging consensus. But of course I did and do have skin in the game. And I could almost hear the ticks. I knew I was doing the right thing, and so I chafed at the idea that I should back down from our radical research approach and stick to patient advocacy. What I tried to explain and show was that in my dual role—physician-scientist in training *and* patient— I had no choice but to continue at a breakneck pace, and we were in this position because the status quo hadn't gotten us very far. I understood that I had my professional reputation to lose, but I couldn't bring myself to care. My illness had liberated me from having to follow many of the unwritten rules that regulate medical research. I questioned the status quo, the accepted way of thinking about my disease, and the way research was being done. Being a physician-scientist-patient gave me a unique lens through which to see more than either perspective on its own. I saw clearly that we scientists and physicians are fallible. And I saw that patients had ideas and concerns that needed to be central to our mission.

Indeed, it would be our modus operandi to engage and involve patients a bit differently than many other organizations did. We wanted to know what research questions were important to them. Maybe not too surprisingly, questions important to patients weren't always the same as those for physicians and researchers. Patients focused more on quality of life issues, such as fertility and symptom management to be able to return to work, whereas physicians and researchers wanted to uncover cells, pathways, and proteins that could be targeted to extend survival. So we integrated suggestions from both groups on the CDCN international research agenda. We also connected patients with one another through social media, online discussion boards, and periodic in-person gatherings. I didn't discount for a minute the power of this kind of connection. Meeting another patient in Dr. van Rhee's waiting room years before had given me the boost of confidence and support I needed to keep fighting.

Plus, patients are sometimes a lot more fun to be around. During our first ever patient webinar, I showed a stick figure cartoon of a man dressed as a castle that I had found on Google. I dubbed him Castle Man and suggested him as a possible unofficial logo for the CDCN. But several patients contacted me afterward to say that the Castle Man was way too puny. They explained that there was no way the hypothetical Castle Man could be a stick figure. Given our battle wounds, they explained, he should be a beast! I couldn't have agreed more. We subsequently adopted a Castle Man that was much more Beast-like and shared the new cartoon with patients on another webinar. Two weeks later, a patient posted a photo on Facebook of the Beast-like Castle Man tattooed on his shoulder, the first of many patient body parts to host him. *If this isn't patient engagement,* I thought, *then I don't know what is.* Castleman disease patients had been waiting to come together to fight. They just needed a galvanizing force. I knew that we were going to accomplish big things together.

One patient who was tuned in to that initial webinar would play a particularly large role in our growth. Greg Pacheco and his wife, Charlyn, had founded Castleman's Awareness & Research Effort (CARE) in 2007. Greg and his board had been doing good work around awareness but weren't satisfied to stop there. They wanted to be a part of discovering new treatments and were excited by what they saw of the CDCN vision. Soon thereafter, Greg invited us to merge the CDCN with CARE and move forward under the CDCN name. I know now that this was a rather remarkable offer—and a rarity in biomedical research. More often than merge, research groups and foundations tend to splinter into often competitive subgroups. New families affected by rare diseases tend to start new foundations from scratch even when others exist. As a result, individual rare diseases can often have dozens of organizations working in parallel, often with competing agendas, inconsistent objectives, and fractions of the total funding pool to distribute. Greg and his fellow board members were taking a bold step. They could have chosen to maintain the autonomy and familiarity of the status quo rather than join forces with a laser-focused lunatic like me and my intense colleagues. This was like adding Mr. T and the A-Team to a UN peacekeeping mission: You better be ready for fireworks. They were.

As for Frits van Rhee, Arthur Rubenstein, and my decision? After a little deliberation, our choice was simple: We had a common mission—to cure Castleman disease—and *collaborative* was part of our name. We gladly accepted Greg's offer. We merged.

It was now time to determine our top-priority research studies. After crowdsourcing sixty ideas from the CDCN community, the scientific advisory board combined, tweaked, and ranked the ideas into a prioritized list of twenty study ideas. The top priority: to search for a possible virus that could be causing iMCD. We reasoned that a virus caused one form of MCD (HHV-8-associated MCD) and that viruses are highly capable of inducing immune system hyperactivation like iMCD patients exhibit. And if we could figure out a viral cause, then we could figure out several other unknowns very quickly, such as the key cell types harboring the virus and potential targets for new therapies.

Armed with our top-priority question, we reached out to the top "viral-hunting" researchers in the world. This step followed through on our mission to be proactive. We didn't care if these researchers had ever heard of Castleman disease so long as they had the technical chops to chase down a potential causal virus.

Before overtime: training for Georgetown football, and (below) together with my sisters and parents before heading off for my freshman year at Georgetown (2003).

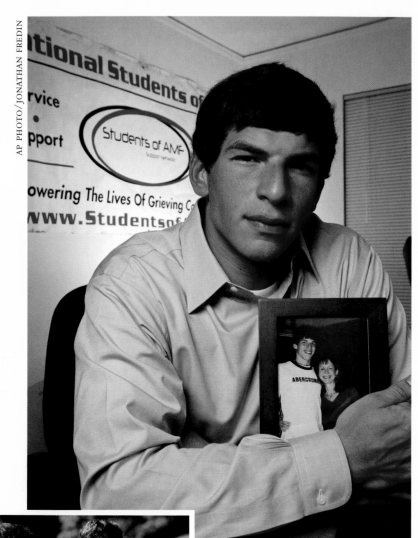

Losing my mother, whose photo I am holding here, was devastating. Starting the AMF support network and holding fundraising events in her honor—like the 2006 Boot Camp 2 Beat Cancer—were the only silver linings.

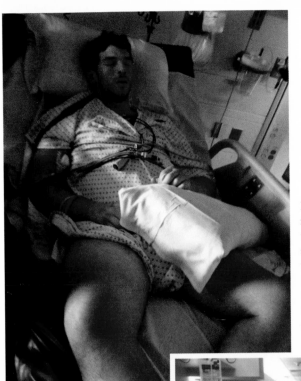

I first became mysteriously sick in the middle of medical school, 2010. With my vital organs failing, I drifted in and out of consciousness. No matter what, though, my dad always had my back.

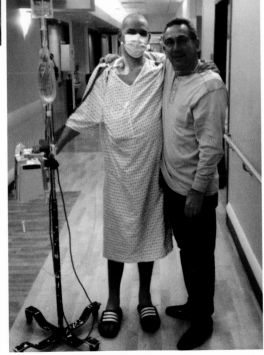

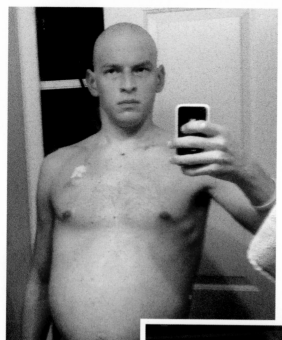

I was finally discharged from the hospital for the first extended period in the spring of 2011, but not before being confused for my dad's pregnant wife because of my distended belly. Despite the circumstances, we laughed hard at that.

A year later, in May 2012, I was back in the hospital with another relapse, but I was optimistic and felt ready for war this time around.

During my relapse in May 2012, I learned that I had run out of treatment options. I promised my family that I would dedicate the rest of my life—however long it might be—to finding a cure for this disease. I got to work studying samples in the lab and building an international collaborative research network.

Chemotherapy spared my life when I relapsed a year later—my fifth near-death episode. Our families and close friends threw Caitlin and me an engagement party a few weeks later. I was bald and weak, but we were together. Now I just needed to discover a new treatment to extend my life so that I could actually marry her . . .

I started out chasing my own cure, but my work today is for the other Castleman disease patients that I have met along the way. Shown here are Katie, who was the second Castleman disease patient ever treated with the drug that I'm on, and Gary, who gave me a first-hand view into how scary it is to watch someone you love battle Castleman disease. They've both generously contributed samples that I have studied in my lab.

Thanks to my Wharton classmates, who rallied behind me when I relapsed during the early days of business school, we have started to turn the tide against Castleman disease. When I was asked to be the student speaker at the 2015 Wharton Commencement, I was so thrilled to be able to formally thank them. It was a very special moment for me.

But we still have a lot of work to do to better understand Castleman disease and the workings of the immune system in myriad other diseases. I work like a maniac and often run out of white board space in my University of Pennsylvania office.

The loves of my life:
Caitlin and our daughter, Amelia.

Our top candidate, the leading expert on this kind of research, who was at Columbia University, agreed to perform the study. However, he would need twenty frozen lymph node samples from iMCD and UCD patients. Lymph nodes are rarely ever frozen after being resected. Thus, we needed biospecimens from a rare subtype of a rare disease preserved in a *very* rare way. So we put the CDCN's network of now more than three hundred members to work, contacting physicians and researchers around the world to see if we could identify these precious samples. After months of outreach, seven institutions based in Japan, the United States, and Norway agreed to contribute twenty-three samples to this study. Altogether, we knew this research would take several years, but it could begin!

I was ready to begin something new now too. Caitlin and I were seeing each other as often as possible—in Philadelphia, in New York, and sometimes in North Carolina, when she traveled with me to get my regular siltuximab and chemotherapy infusions. I had known for years that I wanted to spend the rest of our lives together. Life was better and I was happier with her in it; I knew she felt the same way about me. I had known since seeing her at my bedside during my fourth relapse that I had to stop imagining that future and get on with it! But I still struggled with the decision. I desperately wanted to marry Caitlin, and I knew she wanted to marry me, but was it asking too much of her? The man she'd started dating years before—a carefree quarterback with seemingly full control of his future—was not the man she was with now. Now, I was a critically ill patient fighting for each new day. Now, I was a scientist chasing after life with no guarantees. As ready as I was to propose, I also thought about breaking up with her and pushing her away from me, so that she could find a more stable and predictable and easier life with someone else. She deserved that. But I knew she would refuse and that this would only hurt her worse. I had already denied her twice before. I couldn't do it a third time. And I wanted so much to be her husband. I started to shop for an engagement ring.

I chose December 16, 2012, as the date I would propose. Caitlin would be visiting and I told her that we had brunch reservations at a restaurant near our favorite park in Philadelphia. I arranged for our families and friends to gather at the nearby restaurant, from which they could see us in the park and at which I hoped Caitlin and I would join them to celebrate after she said yes. On the way out of my apartment, I stopped by the mailroom and "found" a card from my then seven-year-old niece, Anne Marie. I gave it to Caitlin as we walked across the park.

The front of the card was adorned with multicolor stick figure drawings of Caitlin, Anne Marie, and me. Inside, it read:

> *Dear Aunt Caitlin,*
> *I am so excited for the wedding and can't wait for you to be a part of our family.*
> > *Love,*
> > *Anne Marie*
> *P.S. I'm a really good flower girl!*

Involving Anne Marie in my plan felt important, because she and Caitlin were very close. But I now retell this part of the story with a wink and a grin: Even if Caitlin was unsure about saying yes to me, she wouldn't want to let Anne Marie down. Because even though I thought we were on the proverbial same page about marriage, I *was* nervous about this dramatic moment. Caitlin covered her mouth with her hands. She was completely shocked.

She said yes. We both cried tears of joy.

Once we'd recovered our poise, we walked to the restaurant

to join our families and friends in celebration. Alone together at the end of that amazing day, we spent some time discussing what we'd do next. She was working in fashion in New York but was ready to leave. I was in the throes of medical school with a semester to go, working in the hospital every day, and couldn't leave Philadelphia. Before she got on her train to New York that evening, Caitlin decided that she'd give three months' notice to her employer right away and move to Philadelphia to live with me. She'd begin looking for jobs in Philadelphia. We both agreed that we needed at least a year before our wedding so that Caitlin had time to focus on relocating and finding a job before wedding planning ramped up too much. We were so excited!

But the excitement wouldn't last for long. A week after our engagement, I had my every-six-month PET/CT scan. This time, I did it when I was supposed to. In addition to looking for iMCD activity, PET/CT scans also search the body for cancer, which iMCD patients are at an increased risk for developing. The scan showed that I had a tumor growing in my liver with increased metabolic activity, potentially indicating cancer. My doctors felt that it was probably just a giant ball of blood vessels, like those hemangiomas on my skin, and not actually cancer. Nothing to worry about. We should just rescan in six months, they said. Wait and see. I remember thinking, *Why the hell do we do these tests if we disregard the results when they come back abnormal?* I had been burned enough times before by human error, physician misinterpretation, and personal avoidance. I wasn't just going to hope that it was a ball of blood vessels and trust my doctors' judgment. Especially now that I had a wedding in my future. Surprisingly, I wasn't afraid. I had learned from my previous experiences that there is no reason to spend energy worrying about an unknown. You might worry much more—or even far less—than you should. I reasoned that it's far better to spend that energy trying to figure out what the hell is going on. Hyperfocusing on a diagnosis completely pushed out any space for nervousness. Caitlin and I continued to see each other every weekend. We talked about what this could mean, but following my lead, Caitlin remained fairly stress-free. I got a second opinion and pushed for another scan, an MRI, to be done a couple weeks later. In just those few weeks, the tumor had doubled in size. It was growing fast. An understatement: This was not a good sign. The scan also confirmed that it definitely wasn't a giant ball of blood vessels and it wasn't going to just go away with hope—it's a good thing I was done hoping.

A subsequent biopsy revealed that I now had a rare form of cancer called an EML4-ALK-rearranged inflammatory myofibroblastic tumor in addition to my iMCD. At first, I was terrified, though I was also so exhausted and battle-weary from my fight against iMCD that I could barely get the energy up to show my panic. Then, I turned to Google. *What is an inflammatory myofibroblastic tumor?* In just a few minutes, my terror turned to optimism! Inflammatory myofibroblastic tumors, or IMTs, can release inflammatory molecules like IL-6, turn on the immune system, and cause symptoms just like those seen in Castleman disease! *Maybe I didn't have the bad luck of being struck by both iMCD and an IMT. Maybe the IMT had been in my liver all along and was the source of all my problems. Maybe it wasn't on top of my iMCD. Maybe it was what turned on my immune system, which led to my iMCD in the first place. Maybe we could cut it out and my nightmare with iMCD would be gone forever! Maybe this was the missing puzzle piece for all iMCD patients!*

The surgery would be intense, so Caitlin moved up her last day of work by a couple weeks, and moved in with me. She was the last person I saw before I went under on my twenty-eighth birthday. We were both scared, but I was also ready for the IMT to come out and possibly bring an end to my battle with iMCD.

Five hours and three units of blood later, 15 percent of my liver—including the cancer—was carefully resected. I had a ten-inch abdominal battle wound to show for it. And the pain to accompany it. The epidural that should have given me relief during recovery had not been properly placed, so I could feel everything when I woke up. There isn't a scale from one to ten or an appropriate frowny face to describe the pain. I had had my abdominal muscles dissected, a chunk of my liver wedged out, and the remainder of the liver torched with an argon laser, which is basically a flamethrower, to stop the internal bleeding. I watched the clock all night, waiting for the moments every fifteen minutes that I could push the button to administer more pain medication into my veins, but even then I felt seemingly everything. The next morning, a new epidural was placed and the stabbing pain dissipated.

Soon after I got my new epidural, the surgeon came into my room to inform me that based on careful review of the margins of the resected tumor, a small amount of the cancer had been inadvertently left in my liver. I tried to sit up a bit in the bed to make sure I had heard him correctly, but contracting my abdomen felt like being stabbed with a sword. *Wait, what? You didn't get the whole thing out? You closed me up before you confirmed the borders were clear? This is Surgical Oncology 101!* I wanted to scream. Instead, I took a deep breath and then quietly but insistently pleaded with him to go back in for the rest of the cancer. Unfazed by my begging, he told me I couldn't handle another surgery in my state and that the argon laser had likely killed any remaining cancer cells that may have been left behind. I was exhausted from all of the highs and lows. I relented and put my luck in the argon laser's hands.

As soon as I was well enough, I returned to the hospital to review my previous scans with radiologists to see if this was the missing puzzle piece. *Could the liver cancer be the cause of my iMCD and have been there all along? Most directly, did they see any signs of the tumor in previous scans?* But no matter how close we looked, we couldn't see any indication that it was there during my previous episodes. I rationalized that maybe it was just too small to see before, but it actually *was* there all along, underlying this disease. *Now it's gone and maybe my iMCD won't come back,* I mused. I knew it was a stretch.

My disease's relentless relapses and now this rather dramatic and health-weakening cancer episode—and in the larger scheme of things, it really did feel like just an episode—had forced my outlook for the future to be quite myopic. I rarely scheduled anything more than three weeks in the future, the interval between my siltuximab infusions. But I was able to complete my final few rotations in time to walk in medical school graduation in May 2013. That was such a happy occasion, and my family—including Caitlin's parents and brother—gathered to celebrate.

I'd worked a long, long time to earn the right to my next step: medical residency. But suddenly something else held more appeal.

At this point, I had identified the key unanswered questions in the iMCD field, crowdsourced the key studies to answer these questions, and begun to build the infrastructure to advance these research studies, but there was a lot of work still to do and a lot of refinement that could help speed things along. I wanted to explore how these steps could help other rare diseases. Strange as it seemed to many, I decided that business school was what I needed to tackle next. At first, I felt guilty for not going directly to residency, as medical school graduates are expected to do. But here again almost dying had liberated me, this time to do exactly what I wanted to do—right now. My rationale: The research challenges I needed to overcome to save my life and others weren't as often rooted in medicine as in business, strategy, and management. I wanted to optimize the collaborative network approach I was building for Castleman disease. I also needed to keep pushing my iMCD research forward. The clock was ticking, and residency would have slowed down each of these pursuits.

In retrospect, I see that my decision to put residency on hold in favor of an MBA also demonstrated my newfound interest in and passion for research over clinical medicine. I felt that in medicine, I would have to hope the drugs at my disposal would be able to save a life and rely on existing data to guide my decisions. In research, I could generate the data and the discoveries that lead to a drug that could save a life—perhaps thousands— and insights into why a drug may or may not work. I would use business school to pick up the skills I needed to overcome hurdles in biomedical research and iterate on my approach to make research more efficient, collaborative, and strategic for Castleman disease and, I hoped, many more rare diseases.

I would begin my MBA studies at Wharton in the fall.

CHAPTER FOURTEEN

"WELL . . . because it's a really interesting disease. So little is known. These patients deserve better. Patients . . . who have the disease."

"Yeah, I get that, but why did you pick . . . what's it called—"

"Castleman disease."

"Yeah, Castleman disease. Seems kind of random. Do you have a personal connection to it or something?"

"I got introduced to it in med school."

These were the kinds of conversations I was having when I got to business school. I couldn't come out and tell the whole truth. I was happy and eager to tell people that I was here to do an MBA to develop the skills I'd need to accelerate research and drug development for Castleman disease, but I couldn't tell *my* story.

It wasn't a deep mystery why.

I was proud: I just didn't want to be treated differently. I didn't want to be that "sick guy." Like the kid at summer camp with the asthma inhaler whom the counselors always kept on the sidelines. Only in this case, with a disease that none of them would recognize or understand—after all, the medical community barely understood it. My med school friends knew me before I was sick, and they stuck with me afterward. But I had never made new friends as the sick guy. Before I got sick, I was always the helper, the supporter. I liked that role; it's something I clearly inherited from my mom. I didn't like being the one in need of help. I realized I was experiencing something that many of my patients had known intimately. It's *different* being sick, apart from the vagaries of the actual sickness. It makes you different. In ways that can very quickly feel unfair.

I was afraid: There really were vulnerabilities to my being sick. As I'd discovered at the medical meeting where I'd been instructed to speak only as a patient—not as a researcher—being sick changed people's expectations of me. Some people would especially doubt my objectivity. They'd reject my ambition to be a leader in a field precisely *because* I had so much skin in the game. But I knew in my heart that my personal stake in figuring out how this disease worked and how to stop it would actually make me more rigorous in my approach. I wouldn't stop at a result that was just statistically significant or one that could be published in a medical journal. I would keep going. I would have to. My goal wasn't tenure, or a big grant, or a medal. My goal was staying alive and saving others with my disease. I would keep validating my findings with experiment after experiment after experiment until I believed my interpretations were true enough to save myself and others. Still, if I revealed my underlying interest in Castleman disease, I thought that my motivation would remain suspect.

And, I can see now, I was indeed naïve. I continued to believe that our relatively small volunteer CDCN team, made up of a few classmates from medical school and a few patients and loved ones, had the needed skills and the necessary bandwidth to accelerate work in a field that had been crawling forward for six decades. We had a lot of work to do to execute our ambitious research agenda and effectively engage hundreds of physicians, researchers, and patients. I did recognize that my new classmates' skills and knowledge could greatly help us, especially with fundraising and external—outside the CDCN network—communications, which were basically nonexistent. But here again, my fear of being "outed" kept me from recruiting any of them to join the CDCN fight. I was silent on social media. I even deleted old Facebook photos and online articles that mentioned my illness, so that these new business school friends wouldn't find out about my health. And my trips every three weeks to North Carolina for siltuximab were "to visit family" (which was not untrue). I just worked my tail off in secret and hoped that our outmatched crew could make the necessary progress on our own.

You'd think I would have been smarter about all of this: less proud, less afraid, more realistic. After all, by now, I thought I had a pretty good grasp on hope. I thought I'd seen through some of its pathologies. I'd learned how to activate it, and how to tell the kind of hope that *pacifies* you from the kind of hope that inspires you to work. But I didn't see the proverbial light. Hiding my illness may have made tactical sense in one social situation or another, but it put me in a position of siloing my Castleman disease work from the rest of my life.

As much of a misstep as my secrecy was, it bore some kind of imperfect fruit.

I had been meticulously tracking my daily symptoms in a small black notebook. Fatigue: No. Appetite: Good. Enlarged lymph nodes: No. Blood moles: None. And I aggregated data from my weekly blood tests in an Excel spreadsheet. Everything was looking good for me. And now I was also sneaking in visits to the Translational Research Laboratory at Penn in between classes and team projects to analyze the results of blood tests and lymph node studies on my own samples and others and to consume as many medical articles as possible. Alone in my self-imposed silo, I was shocked by what I was finding. It started to dawn on me that the medical community had iMCD all wrong. Not *just* wrong; the accepted understanding was upside down.

The penny dropped for me one day as I pored over images of lymph nodes from patients with autoimmune diseases, such as lupus and rheumatoid arthritis. The lymph nodes had a set of features almost identical to those taken from people with Castleman disease. In Castleman disease, these enlarged lymph nodes and characteristic abnormalities are considered to represent the initiating factors of the disease and the source of the IL-6. In other words, Castleman disease had always been classified as a "lymph node disorder," in which the enlarged lymph nodes caused the problems by producing excess IL-6, which then led to hyperactivation of the immune system. From there it was a straight line to organ dysfunction of the liver, kidneys, bone marrow, heart, lungs, and so on.

In lupus, however, enlarged lymph nodes are accepted as a *reaction* or *effect* of the disease: The immune system gets hyperactivated, often due to incorrectly recognizing normal tissue as foreign invaders; immune cells proliferate and produce excessive inflammatory signals (including IL-6); and these *then* lead inevitably to organ dysfunction and sometimes enlarged lymph nodes.

After reviewing the images, I called Arthur Rubenstein to share what I had observed and what I was wondering: Could it be that in iMCD, as in lupus, the enlarged lymph nodes and their unusual features are an outcome of the disease, rather than its cause? Could this be an immune system disorder first and foremost, not a lymph node disorder?

This may seem like a simple distinction. But the order of operations was and is all-important. Misidentifying the symp-

tom for the cause of iMCD could, I reasoned, be the reason its
cure remained a mystery. Maybe we were treating it totally
wrong—like treating chicken pox with acne medication.

From what I could tell, interpreting the lymph nodes as the
problem had become established wisdom through some pretty
specious reasoning. Some people were frankly making the case
that enlarged lymph nodes must be the origin *because all iMCD
patients have enlarged lymph nodes with these characteristic changes.*
But that's like saying that firefighters must cause all fires because
you always find firefighters near fires. We know better.

The firefighting metaphor can be taken further. The lymph
node really is like the firehouse of the immune system: It's where
the cells of the immune system go to communicate with one
another, train together, and prepare for dispatch. And we know
from other immune system conditions that lymph nodes enlarge
as a response to immune hyperactivation. Any time of day, and
under any circumstances, the cells get the call and assemble in
the lymph nodes to coordinate their response.

And the singular focus on IL-6 as the only factor leading to
the signs and symptoms experienced by iMCD patients also did
not seem to be supported by the data, sparse as they were. Sure,
IL-6 was elevated in some patients, and blocking IL-6 helped a
portion of patients too—including some with low or normal
IL-6 levels—but there were also patients in whom blocking IL-6
did not work. And when IL-6 levels were low or normal in
iMCD patients, like me, the results were simply considered to
be incorrect. But the coordinated research to develop the panoptic IL-6 test had not revealed any higher IL-6 levels than the
traditional tests had. Maybe IL-6 levels didn't have to be elevated
in the blood to be critical to driving the disease in some patients.
Or maybe IL-6 wasn't the problem for everyone and there were
other cytokines, which just hadn't been measured, that were
driving the disease in those patients. So, I began to propose that
"IL-6" be replaced with "cytokines" in my new model and con-

tinued to push forward studies to systematically measure the levels of more cytokines in iMCD patients.

The difference between the old and accepted hypothesis and my new one wasn't just an interesting intellectual puzzle. It had everything to do with treatment—and was possibly the reason why none of mine had really worked so far. According to the old model, iMCD should be treated with either chemotherapy to wipe out the cells composing the lymph node tissue or infusions of siltuximab to block IL-6. Well, I was living proof—for the time being—that going after these targets with these treatments wasn't the right approach for all of us; my iMCD kept coming back.

Instead, and if it all came down to a hyperactive immune system, as I suspected (even if we didn't know why it was hyperactive), we should be trying so-called immunosuppressants. These are the drugs that people take after receiving liver, kidney, and other organ transplants to stop their immune systems from attacking their potentially lifesaving but foreign new organ. Immunosuppressants weaken the cells of the immune system so they can't inflict as much damage, for good or for evil, whereas chemotherapy kills everything in its path. And they're a hell of a lot easier to take than chemotherapy. I was also keenly aware that my current treatment regimen matched the old model, but I wasn't sad at the prospect of leaving behind the "carpet bomb" mentality of treatment. I was still getting siltuximab every three weeks and chemotherapy every week. It sucked. It's hard to get more specific than that. Nausea doesn't inspire eloquence. But I didn't have any alternatives just yet.

I proposed four possible causes for the immune hyperactivation for future research: a virus (like in HHV-8-associated MCD), a cancerous cell population (like in POEMS-associated MCD), an inherited genetic mutation (as seen in autoinflammatory disorders), and self-reactive B and/or T cells (as seen in autoimmune conditions). I shared my new theory with some colleagues in the CDCN community I was assembling—and didn't get a particularly encouraging response. I wasn't necessarily surprised. Even though the CDCN was a novel creation, my colleagues were still all coming to the project with their existing perspectives. Most had years of irreplaceable experience and a traditional introduction to disease research. But, frankly, I was different. I had been well on the way to joining the establishment—but a funny thing happened.

Getting Castleman disease didn't give my words moral weight. It didn't make me "more right" about anything. It didn't turn me into a superhero. What it did was push me off the beaten path—and right into a ditch. From there, things looked a little different.

A part of my ability to bounce back from the agonizingly repetitive Castleman disease attacks was in my focusing on what I was gaining. My disease was terribly peculiar—indeed, that was a part of the problem. But peculiarity has its benefits. In a different context, peculiarity might be mistaken for originality. Originality is the handmaiden of creativity. Silicon Valley has been imploring us to "think outside the box" for decades. If you can get outside the box through peaceful means, or meditation, that's terrific. But even if you get outside the box via multiple bouts of organ failure, hey, it counts.

I was gaining an ability to see things from an angle—and with an urgency—almost no one else had. I felt this new perspective was starting to pay off, even if select others didn't yet share my view.

I understood that I now needed to get my hypothesis and supporting information out to the world and that, ironically, I'd have to go the 100 percent traditional route to reach that goal: I needed to publish my proposed conclusions in a hematology journal, the way research has been done for centuries. First, because the best solutions are arrived at only after they've undergone intense scrutiny, I knew that I needed to share the data with colleagues who could criticize and poke holes in my logic. I reviewed it with Chris Nabel, my friend who was helping with the CDCN and iMCD research on nights and weekends while taking a hiatus from medical school to get a PhD. He found flaws, we worked together to fix them, and he contributed to the first version of the paper. Now would come the ultimate test: sharing it with Dr. Frits van Rhee.

When I traveled to Little Rock for my next checkup with Frits—as I was now calling him—I brought copies of the papers and data on my laptop that supported this new model for understanding iMCD. He wasn't surprised to see me parsing through documents and typing on my laptop when he came into the exam room. That was something he'd grown used to. After we got through the history and physical exam, I broke out my notes. I could tell he was choosing his words so as to not knock the wind out of my sails: He was interested, he said, but skeptical.

The next six months involved many conference calls with Chris and Frits after my business school classes, and hours of rewriting drafts, synthesizing findings from the literature, scrapping, and writing some more. We had lots of disagreements; no one held back. This could have been awkward considering Frits had saved my life multiple times and Chris was a good friend. But our disagreements were all in the spirit of getting it right; and we all knew that. After more than a year of steady work and my stabilized health, we were nearly ready to submit the paper for publication. It included an appropriate balance of historical understanding, new possibilities, and future directions. It was bold: We proposed a uniform terminology system for all subtypes of Castleman disease, a new framework for researching and treating iMCD, and hypotheses for the cause of iMCD. This would serve as the foundation upon which all of our future research studies would be based and for the hypotheses that we would test. And the uniform terminology system would serve as the common language that we would all speak. It was a lot and, frankly, ambitious. Arthur Rubenstein (I was still turning to him every week or two for advice) suggested we submit our work to the top hematology journal in the world, *Blood*. We just had a few more tweaks left to make.

Even though I worried about not being taken seriously as a researcher because of my patient status, I can admit that if I hadn't been a patient myself with no idea how much longer I had in overtime four, I don't know if I would have had the brass to propose such a radical shift in thinking at such an early stage in my career. The hierarchical—and often arbitrary—rules of medicine dictate that senior researchers propose these models and synthesize primary data into review articles that summarize the state of thinking, especially review articles in journals like *Blood*. But having the disease and knowing that I wouldn't survive without solutions—now—liberated me from this entrenched tradition.

I love medicine. I think all doctors do, even those who get burned out.

I love parsing through available evidence to guide decisions. But Castleman disease made me realize that I love generating data and coming up with solutions more than anything. I was losing patience waiting for other people to generate the data needed to lead to the solutions. I needed new strategies to create more data to lead to more solutions more quickly.

In other words—I was starting to really benefit from my MBA coursework.

It felt great to be back in the classroom, back in the library, back in the books. I was flexing all new learning muscles while digesting case examples of effective collaborations in nonmedical industries, principles of strategic planning, tools for optimizing efficiency, the economics of drug development, and negotiation strategies. I was particularly drawn to the organizational psychologist and Wharton professor Adam Grant's philosophical model of givers and takers, or the styles that we all bring to our interactions (it occurred to me that there were surprisingly a whole lot of takers in research). And I was inspired by the idea of crowdsourcing through what are known as innovation tournaments. It was impossible to learn about all of these exciting ways to unlock potential and not see how rigid medicine so often was. Even on the research side of things.

It became even clearer to me that the approach in biomedical research of *let's hope the right researcher with the right skill set applies to perform the right study at the right time* was backward. Not just because it was inefficient and hopeless—but because I was learning how many alternative ways of doing things there were! There's no sweeter discovery to someone with a rare illness, I promise you.

Most important, I was learning that innovation isn't an art. Innovation, like hope itself, is a force. Innovations are most effectively made with the following systematic approach: inventorying all possible ideas from a wide range of stakeholders, systematically evaluating and prioritizing them, recruiting the very best people in the world, and then working like mad to execute. Sound familiar? In my finance class and others, professors often repeated "hope is not a strategy." *So why,* I thought, *is it okay in biomedical research, where the stakes are so high?*

More than a year had passed since my last relapse, and I continued to keep my health history a secret from my new business school cohorts. But suddenly, I didn't have a choice. The siltuximab combined with weekly doses of three chemotherapies, which had been part of the cocktail that had induced multiple responses for me, couldn't keep the iMCD from coming back. Elevated CRP levels, growing blood moles, crashing platelet counts, enlarging lymph nodes in my neck, drenching night sweats. Here Castleman disease was again—for the fifth unbelievable, excruciatingly terrifying time.

This fifth flare also put to rest any lingering suspicion—or hope—that my real problem underlying the iMCD was my liver cancer. There was no way it could be, because it had been removed eight months prior, and an MRI confirmed that the cancer hadn't come back. It'd only been a comforting scapegoat.

Next to the possibility that I could die was the possibility that—even if I lived—my life would continue to be punctuated by these horrible episodes. Episodes that tore me away from my life, from my work, from my friends, from Caitlin. And that brought me closer to death with each bout. It was agonizing if I stopped to think about it.

So I didn't stop to think about it.

If I'm honest with myself, I have to admit I knew this was coming. The liver cancer was an unlikely cause, and the research I had done for the last year suggested that my treatment approach wasn't going to be able to prevent an iMCD relapse. Fortunately, the year's worth of data from my monthly blood tests and my new way of thinking about iMCD would come in very handy. And I also now had an international network of colleagues and scientists to tap into. The liver cancer kerfuffle had finally pushed me over the edge and shown me that I had the power to take charge of my care. I would no longer just rely on my physicians and hope that they'd get it right. I don't mean that with any malice. It wasn't their fault that there was too little known. Just as I had set out to transform the research field in overtime four, I would need to take command of my own treatment this time. It was impossible for me to imagine lying back and becoming just an object again, just a *body*. And a failing body, at that.

I was experiencing crushing fatigue (yet again) and organ failure, but to the extent I was able, I jumped into action. I took a leave from business school but took with me what I'd learned.

I went into what I think of as Entrepreneurial Treatment Mode. My newly minted physician-friends Grant and Duncan, who were also both pursuing MBAs at Wharton, spent hours on the phone with me discussing the plan of attack, scenarios, data, and potential treatments. Grant was especially helpful during this time because he had a habit that bordered on obsessive: Every time anyone ever said the word *can't,* Grant would reply "Why not?" Seriously. Every time. In almost any situation. It wasn't a childlike, sassy response. Just the opposite. He simply has an innate and constant skepticism of the wisdom of the status quo, an insatiable desire for solutions. Real solutions.

With my new attitude, Grant's antiauthoritarianism, and Duncan's do-anything-for-a-friend credo, we made quite the dynamic trio. We vowed that everything—everything—should be on the table, in terms of treatment. No conventional wisdom would go unscrutinized. We didn't care if the solution required a traditional or a nontraditional approach. In hindsight, Alexander the Great and his solution for the Gordian knot comes to mind. As the story goes, an oracle declared that any man who could unravel the complex knot was destined to become ruler of all of Asia. Countless men tried and failed. When Alexander the Great struggled to untie the knot, he drew his sword and sliced it in half. Problem solved. Prophecy fulfilled.

Armed with our collective fighting spirit, we considered every drug that had ever been approved by the FDA for any use—from cancer to constipation. A drug may have been created to target a parasite or a receptor to decrease heartburn, but we asked what else it could do. Could one of these drugs previously approved for another disease be the magic bullet for me?

If a drug existed that we thought could work, we'd get our hands on it. It's useful to have a medical degree. And a network of physicians and scientists in your contact list.

In a way, the timing was on our side: When I was in remission, we could try all the new treatments we wanted to, but we wouldn't really know if they were working until I relapsed or didn't. It was only during one of these relapses that we had adequate test conditions. When all of my organs were failing, we could try a new drug and know very quickly if my organ function improved—i.e., whether it worked.

Of course, we also understood that my time was limited: The window of opportunity was small. If the drugs didn't work, I would die. So, if a new drug wasn't working fast enough, we needed to try to preserve enough time for the combination chemo to have a last chance.

To start, though, we knew we needed to identify a few candidate cell types, cellular communication lines, or proteins that were abnormally increased or decreased during my episodes and possibly critical to the disease to try to target with a drug. Breast cancer innovations are examples of what's possible when you can do this. One of the biggest breakthroughs in breast cancer was the identification of HER2 on the surface of breast cancer tumors. Once it was clear that the protein was essential to the cellular survival of some cases of breast cancer, drugs were developed that are highly effective if a patient's particular breast cancer overexpresses this protein. We needed to find a similar "target" in my iMCD. Unfortunately, we had a number of hurdles: We didn't know what cell type to go after out of hundreds of possibilities, the surface of every cell looks like a forest filled with thousands of proteins to choose from, and the inside of each cell is made up of thousands of proteins interconnected through countless communication lines that could be targeted too. And each cell type—let alone each protein—could take years to study.

Still, we used what we had. In the data I had assembled for the paper I was getting ready to submit to *Blood,* I looked for candidate cell types, communication lines, or proteins to target. From there, we searched drug databases to see if any existing

FDA-approved drugs—regardless of the diseases they were approved to treat—were known to act on these potential targets.

We considered additional criteria as well. Among these potential drugs, we needed to filter out ones that would be slow to show an effect. In an ideal scenario, we'd perform a large study on many patients in which each patient would be randomly assigned to receive one of these drugs, and we'd identify the best treatment. But we didn't have that luxury. We had only one patient, multiple drugs, and very little data. So we also needed to consider the potential chronology of administering drugs so that one drug's effect in me wouldn't confound our interpretation of the effectiveness of a subsequent drug. We needed to balance the chronology with the likelihood of success for each drug to inform our decision. But without any actual data on the effectiveness of these drugs in iMCD to guide us, the probabilities we used were only our best guesses.

Last, we needed to account for the side effect profile of each drug. It's easier to take a drug with terrible side effects if you know it could work. When you have nothing to indicate it will work, you want to limit potential side effects, which can include death.

I wanted a clear treatment plan so desperately. It feels so great when your doctor has all the answers. No questions. In any other context, the unilaterality might come off as disrespectful. Not in the doctor's office. A doctor's speed and confidence are comforting. The speed means she knows exactly what to do, she's seen this a thousand times, and everything will be fine. You can look at her diplomas on the wall as evidence that the decision was well-informed. You can grab on to the success stories that nurses share about the patients who came back from the dead. You can believe that you've been sent to this doctor by a higher power for a reason: to get better. You can pray that your physician will be directed to the correct choice.

It's absolutely terrifying when you have to figure it out yourself. What if this choice doesn't work and the second choice would have been the answer? What if I overlooked something that could have swayed me to the right choice? What if my data were wrong? What if my way of thinking was wrong? After all the research, publications, debates with experts, diagrams, and decision trees, there's no answer key at the end. Ultimately, it was on no one's shoulders but my own. And my life depended on being right. It would have helped if I had continued my training in a medical residency or was actually practicing as a physician. My limited experiences taking care of patients as a medical student left me severely ill-equipped for these kinds of decisions.

In a word, I was scared. But I understood that you can choose which fear you'll face. When I was still a participant in the Santa Claus theory of civilization, I was just a little kid waiting for a miracle. Little kids are really good at waiting for good things to happen. They're also really good at waiting for terrible things to happen. Maybe at night, in bed, when the rhododendron scraping at the window starts to sound a whole lot like claws. What do you do then? Pull the covers up a bit tighter and . . . wait until morning. If you're feeling especially intrepid, maybe you go wake your parents up. But, then again, the hallway has terrors of its own.

The other kind of fear is the kind that comes right before a football game. Yes, those guys are afraid. I know they don't ever admit it (except when they've been retired for a decade, own a few car dealerships, and don't need to be tough guys anymore). But they are. We all were. But the fear is met with and stirs up a lot of other feelings. It's the kind of fear that forces you to act—to run through the game plan in your head, to remember the game tape, to think about the opponent's weak cornerback, whose foot positioning gives away his coverage on every play. Instead of being like the child who has basically two options— freeze or go get help—the football player plans. He's got a say in things. And he channels his fear into action.

Fear can paralyze. It can also focus.

This relapse was the first time I'd have a chance to test my new hypothesis: that iMCD was an immune hyperactivation disorder, not a lymph node disorder. All things aside, that was exciting. I loved the idea of collecting as much information as possible from my relapse and treatment so that our future research would have some solid clinical evidence to build on. I had a lymph node biopsy performed and blood samples collected for future testing. I was putting my body, piece by piece, into the lab. And I was putting together a ranked list of about twenty possible treatment options. I wasn't slashing, but I was whittling away at a solution.

Blood tests from each of my previous relapses indicated that T cells were highly activated. T cells are a specialized type of immune cell and key weapons in the body's immune arsenal known for their ability to cause destruction (including when being reprogrammed by researchers into CAR T cells and directed at cancer, as I mentioned earlier, but also when attacking healthy tissue). We decided that the next drug I tried should target them. The immunosuppressant cyclosporine was known to be able to weaken these cells, and it was FDA-approved to prevent organ transplant rejection. I had even heard of a doctor in Japan—a member of the CDCN—who had tried it with some success in a couple of iMCD patients. I emailed that doctor to get additional information. Compared against the other drugs on my list, it seemed like a promising choice: It targeted activated T cells, had the potential for a fairly quick turnaround, and had a mostly tolerable side effect profile.

I presented my plan to my family and Caitlin. They asked surprisingly few questions and weren't interested in the details. They just wholeheartedly trusted I was on the right track. If only I could share their confidence. Finally, I called my doctor who had been overseeing my siltuximab infusions in North Carolina to see what he thought. There was a long pause.

"Considering the limited options at this point and the ineffectiveness of the drugs we've tried, I think it makes sense." He liked that cyclosporine had been used in Japan with some success and that the side effects weren't too bad. The prescription was ready that very afternoon. I wasn't totally confident it would work, but my other options didn't seem to be any better.

The dramatic improvement I had hoped for didn't come. I didn't get any better. But I didn't get any worse. Before the cyclosporine, my CRP levels had risen over a few days from 4 to 10 to 40 (I wouldn't be fooled again by the wrong units: the upper limit of normal was, in fact, 10). Since I had started cyclosporine, it was hovering between 35 and 45 on daily blood tests instead of climbing above 100, as it had each time before. My fatigue, night sweats, and fevers also maintained fairly constant intensity but didn't seem to escalate. Considering the typical explosiveness of my disease, we posited that this plateau meant the drug was helping. So we waited. But in a few days, as each time before, my fatigue and blood tests started to worsen.

Emboldened a bit by the fact that my first choice wasn't *flat-out* wrong, I suggested that we add another treatment, intravenous immunoglobulin, or IVIg. It wasn't a great choice on its own, but I thought it could be a good add-on. Intravenous immunoglobulin has the dual ability to decrease immune hyperactivation and protect the body from infections. And it doesn't kill any cells in the lymph nodes or elsewhere, it just has the ability to tamp down immune activation. So if it worked, the success would suggest that immune system activation was the underlying culprit, not something intrinsic to my enlarged lymph nodes.

I felt better within hours of the IVIg infusion. The fatigue subsided. The nausea passed.

I resisted celebrating. I considered the possibility that my mind was tricking my body: the placebo effect. I considered the reality that it was unlikely I'd just unlocked a secret of a disease that had stymied researchers for decades.

But the improvements in my blood tests were dramatic and undeniable. My level of CRP—the greatest marker of my disease and a sign of inflammation—had plummeted from 42 to below 10, back to normal. I had never seen such a large improvement in CRP in such a short period of time. I'd seen it worsen by that much that quickly but had never seen it improve this way, because it is very difficult to completely neutralize whatever is causing such intense inflammation. Remarkably, these results suggested that we had done that here. And other abnormal laboratory tests, like platelet count, albumin, hemoglobin, and kidney function, all returned to normal ranges. Except for some fatigue and night sweats, I was *normal* again. And for the very first time, we'd reversed my relapse without chemotherapy.

Sitting with Caitlin in our apartment living room and reviewing the numbers, I wept with happiness—for myself, for Caitlin, and for everyone down in Arkansas, everyone who had been in touch to share stories and information about the disease in their own lives.

The case was far from closed, but it was starting to get very, very interesting. This was bad news for Castleman disease.

I was even well enough to attend the 2013 American Society of Hematology meeting in New Orleans one week later. This was the same meeting where, a year earlier, we had convened the first CDCN gathering. This time we had forty-five physicians and researchers from around the world at our CDCN meeting (a new meeting attendance record), and I presented my newly proposed framework for understanding and researching iMCD. I was feeling ecstatic—not only was I healthy but I was also back to being just another researcher again. I relished the chance to be slightly boring and stand in front of a PowerPoint. No more dramatics, no more organ failure. At the end of my talk, I mentioned a "patient" with seemingly relentless iMCD who had recently improved substantially with cyclosporine and IVIg. I continued to not disclose that I was a patient myself for fear that I would be treated differently if that were known. Dr. van Rhee and those who knew I was talking about myself grinned at me from across the room.

While in New Orleans, I attended a research presentation where the final results of the international siltuximab clinical trial of seventy-nine iMCD patients were revealed. It was a huge occasion for the community—but somewhat uncertain in its implications. Dr. van Rhee was the lead investigator, and a number of other CDCN members were involved in the trial. It was the only randomized controlled trial, the gold standard test of efficacy in medicine, ever done in iMCD. This was historic. Just over a third of patients treated with siltuximab achieved a partial or complete response, compared to 0 percent on a placebo. And the drug was very well tolerated, with minimal side effects. The data were clear: Patients got better at a significantly higher rate on siltuximab than with a placebo. This trial would almost certainly lead to FDA approval of siltuximab, which would be the first ever approved treatment for iMCD in the United States and would be huge for our patient community.

But I was saddened that two-thirds of patients didn't seem to improve measurably. I had hoped that my own disappointing response to siltuximab was idiosyncratic. Unfortunately, there were a lot of people like me. I was further surprised to learn that the levels of IL-6 rise in all patients after siltuximab is administered, whether the drug works or not. That "first sign" that the drug was likely to work for me had not actually been anything at all. On the other hand, it seemed like I was on the cusp of a new breakthrough treatment, one that might just be the silver bullet for the unlucky two-thirds. It was hard not to feel like a quarterback again, responsible for the team. Answerable to the team. Now that I was feeling well enough, I was able to spend the week after the convention making final tweaks to the paper for *Blood* with Chris and Frits. Right after I clicked submit on the journal's website and my focus began to recede, fatigue rushed in and another ominous thought returned: *I just hope that all of our work will get out to the world to help other patients, even if I am no longer in it.*

Almost exactly five months before Caitlin and I were planning to get married, the game plan completely fell apart.

Despite the new treatment and my initial improvement during this flare, it all came rushing back a few weeks later. All of it. My CRP rose above 100, and my organ function started to deteriorate once again. The fatigue was crippling. Fluid accumulated in my legs, abdomen, and lungs. I had allowed myself to think I might have beaten the beast, but I hadn't. Once again, I went to the airport, destination Little Rock. This time, I had Caitlin by my side. Once again, my dad and sisters met me there. Once again, my blood counts plummeted. It was just like each time before. This time, however, I experienced a not-so-welcome novelty: I was failing so quickly, I fainted in the elevator at the hospital. My dad and Caitlin caught me on the way down. A fitting metaphor. On Christmas Day 2013, I approached death just as I had four times before. Nausea and vomiting overwhelmed me during brief moments of consciousness. No more time for testing new treatments. It was now really overtime five. We went back to those same damn seven chemotherapies. Deck the halls and drop the bombs.

My dad buzzed a Mohawk for me again. It didn't give me

quite the same bump in my spirits that it had the previous time or that Caitlin and my dad had hoped for. So they went to Target for a fake mini Christmas tree to see if that might lift my mood. All that was left in stock was a ragged hot pink tree. It would have to do.

My blood platelet level was lower than 7,000. That's even lower than it was when Francisco's stethoscope slammed into my forehead. It's less than one-twentieth of the lower level you should have of these tiny cells that circulate to prevent bleeding throughout the body. And so the risk of a fatal, spontaneous brain bleed was constant. The only warning would be an intense headache, and then I'd be gone. Castleman disease would finally have won. My father tried to keep my spirits up by telling jokes. I asked him to stop. I could easily have died if I laughed too hard.

My sisters, my dad, Caitlin, and my mother-in-law, Patty, stood by the door, waiting, hoping for matched platelets to arrive every day so that I could get a transfusion. Fortunately, they did arrive, every day. But even then, we had another hurdle to overcome. We had to blunt my fevers before the platelets could be transfused. Things got primitive. The nurses and my family spent hours cooling my body with ice packs every night.

Strangely, my kidney function didn't deteriorate as much as it had during previous relapses. That meant that as my other organs failed and fever burned through my body, my blood was still filtering somewhat, and my thoughts could remain relatively clear. It was a mixed blessing. There were times when I might have given up some of my cognition, frankly. Thoughts can't do much except exacerbate pain, and it was no consolation that I could still piece together complex thoughts like *Will I make it long enough to marry Caitlin?*

The save-the-date postcards for our wedding were put aside.

Even with all of the transfusions, my platelets remained critically low. The doctor on the hematology unit encouraged me to put together a makeshift will. This recommendation shook all of us. As soon as the doctor left the room and I looked at Caitlin, my mind flashed back to the wife of the first patient I encountered in medical school, on my first day of the psychiatry consult service. I remembered the tears that had dripped down her face, untouched, and eventually made their way in between her hands, where she'd gathered some blanket. And now Caitlin's tears followed a similar path. I had swollen cheeks as a side effect of my medications just like that woman's husband. And soon, I too would likely not have the capacity to make medical decisions for myself. Since Caitlin and I were not married, the nurse witnessing the will would not allow Caitlin to help with it, so my sister Gena offered to write down my last wishes on a blank piece of printer paper. Distraught about my deteriorating health and the implications of my doctor's suggestion, Caitlin and her mom walked out of the room in tears.

I was actually glad that Caitlin had to leave the room, because I had a secret and I needed Gena to make note of it: Right before my second round of combination chemotherapy, I had banked a sperm sample, knowing that my counts would plummet with each subsequent round. I had hoped to use it to have children with Caitlin that we could raise together. I was now acutely aware that my dreams for the future had collapsed. I told Gena about the sample, where it was being stored, and gave her power of attorney over it. I explained to Gena that I hadn't told Caitlin about the sample, because I didn't want her to feel any pressure to use it to have a child with me by in vitro fertilization after I was gone.

I know that sounds crazy, but Caitlin knew how much I had dreamed of having a family with her, and I didn't want her to make any decisions *because* I was sick. Rather, I wanted Gena to know about this sample, just in case Caitlin ever asked her about it. And if she did ask, I wanted Gena to make it available to her. But of course, this wasn't what I really wanted at all. Not by a long shot. What I really wanted was to have a child with Caitlin that we could raise together. Matters like whether I wanted CPR to be performed on me, how I felt about life support, and whom I wanted to receive my limited assets somehow felt much less significant. My sister wrote down everything. Then, the nurse and I signed the paper. As soon as I signed it, my sluggish mind shifted back to the looming possibility of a splitting headache that would signal a fatal brain bleed had begun. I quietly hoped it wouldn't come.

The next morning, it arrived. When I told the nurse and doctor about my headache, they immediately knew what it meant. Soon, I was being rushed down the hall to the CT scanner and the fluorescent ceiling lights flashed before my eyes. I knew this was it. My thoughts fixated on Caitlin and my family. Tears dripped onto my gown. They had tilted my bed all the way upright, so that gravity could help with blood return if there was a brain bleed, just as we had done with my first stroke patient in medical school, who had died in front of me in a similar way. As I returned to thinking about Caitlin and my family and crying, I realized that my ruminations were going on longer than I had expected they would. The scan was done. I was back in my room. I wasn't deteriorating the way I had expected. The scan revealed no signs of a brain bleed, just evidence of a nasty sinus infection, which was likely causing the headache. It was a false alarm.

Once again, the cytotoxic chemotherapy did its vicious job, just in time. After being taken to hell and back, I recovered. I was grateful, but I knew it wasn't a permanent solution—if such a thing even existed for me. I was now even closer to the lifetime max dose of these drugs. There are only so many bombs you can drop on one man, during one lifetime; my liver cancer was possibly born of these health-annihilating treatments. We also knew that the chemo provided only a temporary reprieve from the Castleman disease. I couldn't continue this cycle of remissions and then deadly relapses as soon as my immune system strengthened enough to strike again. I was playing Russian roulette with each relapse and needed to figure out a new approach to prevent them.

My lab tests showed the first signs of improvement on New Year's Eve. We all drank sparkling cider on the three-year anniversary of my being mistaken for my dad's pregnant wife. We even took a walk around the floor to commemorate it. We were asleep by 9:00 P.M. I wanted my life back.

CHAPTER FIFTEEN

THERE'S NO MORE stable cliché in medical fiction than the epiphany.

For decades TV writers especially have seemed transfixed by this magical Archimedean moment: the doctor, squinting in concentration (or rubbing his eyes), leaning back in his chair. Then: His head cocks toward something, a memory made visible by a picture on the wall—a connection!—a realization!—and then a scramble. He clears his desk and begins to scribble. Eureka!

But there's a hard truth about epiphanies: They don't materialize out of thin air. They are not magical moments when your IQ ratchets up ten points. They come from what you've already done, your persistent hard work, and usually after years of it. Just as football had increased my pain tolerance and muscle mass, and these things were key in enduring the early days of my illness (but in ways I could never have imagined), epiphanies come to us in surprising ways, bearing the fruits of labors we've already done.

I desperately needed one.

Once my mind cleared from the last round of chemo, disappointment rushed in to fill in the emptiness.

It wasn't lymphoma; it was worse.

Siltuximab hadn't worked.

It wasn't the liver cancer.

Weekly chemo infusions to prevent a relapse hadn't worked.

Cyclosporine hadn't worked.

Prayer hadn't stopped it.

Hope hadn't prevented it.

And though I'd thought I had a breakthrough—an epiphany—with my new theory of this disease, it still hadn't led to an effective treatment.

I had given it my best shot and Castleman disease won the battle again. The only thing that was keeping me alive was also killing me—the repeated rounds of chemo couldn't last forever. The rhythm of my health was no longer tenable. I no longer wanted to limp toward health, and life.

My disappointment didn't last long. I didn't have time for that. While I was still recovering in my hospital room, my sister Gena and I made a list of all the institutions that had my medical records and leftover biospecimens from the last three and a half years. Then she contacted each of the institutions to have those precious data points and specimens sent to Philadelphia. For too long I'd been relying on a disparate network of institutions to test my blood and sift through my data for anything that might be a clue. It was time to centralize and apply my hyperfocus. I had been hospitalized for the start of my second semester of business school and decided to take the remainder of the semester off. I didn't want to pretend things were back to normal. Until I had a way to reliably fight back, nothing would be normal again.

After being discharged, I went home to Philadelphia and

made my headquarters there. I had two interconnected questions on my mind: Could Caitlin and I realistically keep our May 24, 2014, wedding date, and what treatment should I start on to prevent a relapse? The former was very much dependent on the latter.

I spent weeks working from 6:00 A.M. to midnight, poring through thousands of pages of medical records, CDCN research data, and medical literature on Castleman disease and the immune system. Caitlin was my source of strength and inspiration. After moving to Philadelphia, she had found a sales job in the fashion industry, and fortunately for me, she worked from home. So we both worked from our one-bedroom apartment on days that I wasn't in the lab. We didn't talk very much, but I loved having her near me. Every few hours, I pulled myself out of the matrix to spend time with her. She reminded me to eat and also why I was doing all this: I needed to identify a new drug so that we could get married and have a family together.

I was still stuck on the idea that the immune system was the real site and source of the ultimate target. We knew my immune system was going out of control during relapses—it seemed like the whole system, the entire intricate network of billions of cells, got activated each time, but among all those cells, we still didn't know which type was responsible for initiating or propagating iMCD. Or if not a specific cell type, was there a shared communication line that was turned on across various cell types? Or a single molecule, like IL-6, responsible for initiating or driving the iMCD? There would be no treatment without a target to attack.

So the task before me yet again was to find a target. I started with the data I had used at the beginning of my recent relapse. I added the data that were generated from that flare alongside a very important additional data set—those immunological tests that I had requested monthly for the year leading up to my recent relapse. We knew that the activation levels of various components of my immune system were off the charts at the peak of my relapses' fury. But could we find the spark that ignited the fire if we looked at these levels over time? I was hoping to spot any hint of a pattern, any possible entry point for a new kind of treatment that could prevent another flare. I needed to find a weakness in the defenses of the beast, its Achilles' heel. That meant looking for a pattern in the thousands and thousands of pages of test results, medical journal articles, and reports we'd collected. Something that emerged from the noise, as yet unaccounted for.

It was in a series of test results that I found something significant (at least to my hyperfocused mind). I saw that two things happened in my blood just before I experienced my familiar symptoms. Actually, *months* before the symptoms materialized. The data indicated that well before I experienced any of the fatigue and before any of the organ trouble, my T cells activated in a big way, preparing for a fight even though there was no apparent threat. We'd previously observed the increased T cell activation *during* flares and even targeted them the last go-round, but the improvement was only temporary. That they were ramping up before my symptoms began was very interesting. Simultaneously, levels of a protein called vascular endothelial growth factor, or VEGF, also began to rise in my blood. This protein is instrumental in causing blood vessels to grow, something that didn't seem immediately germane. Perhaps it was just another piece of biological noise and not a true signal—lots of stuff happens in a deteriorating body. But . . . the numbers were striking. The levels of both activated T cells and VEGF were about ten times above what were considered to be the upper limits of the normal range.

But at this point we had looked at the levels of only thirteen immunological factors. Remember: You can see only what you look for in medicine. Laboratory tests don't answer the question *What is wrong?* Laboratory tests answer the question *What is the level of* x? or *Is* y *present?* Then, it's the job of the physician or researcher to piece these individual data points together to determine "what is wrong." *What if there were other key factors that we had missed because we weren't measuring them?*

Those stored blood samples would come in handy. I measured the levels of 315 molecules—most of which were involved in the immune system—in those samples. Again, VEGF and the marker of T cell activation were very elevated, both emerging in the top 5 percent of the most elevated proteins.

Though I had already considered T cells as a potential target during my recent relapse, finding signals for T cell activation before and during relapse in two separate data sets strengthened my conviction. The activation of the T cells also supported my suspicion that immune system hyperactivation was at the root of my iMCD. Perhaps the T cells were involved in the mechanism through which the whole shebang started and spread throughout my body. They certainly had access to all parts of it. But suppression of T cell activation with cyclosporine hadn't made a major difference for me with episode five. Maybe my T cells needed to be suppressed in a different way or something else needed to be hit too.

What about VEGF? I knew quite a bit about this protein because of its crucial role in increasing blood vessels and blood supply for cancers. Decades of research had established the following: Blood vessel growth orchestrated by VEGF is essential to meet the blood supply needs of cancerous tumors. *Could a similar line be present in iMCD?*

I began to piece together a plausible and utterly novel linkage between my symptoms, iMCD, and what I was seeing in the data I'd gathered. And it all started with those irritating and nasty things that the doctors had been imploring me to ignore for years. Those pesky blood moles, which grew when I was sick and shrank when I was well. Vascular endothelial growth factor was likely the signal causing them to grow. A representation on my skin of what was going on throughout my body: uncontrolled blood vessel growth.

In hindsight, the VEGF-iMCD connection had showed its hand early, but none of us had recognized it. It had been quietly revealing itself for years. Missed signs began to pile up in my memory: an internationally renowned hematopathologist, Dr. Elaine Jaffe, saying to me once that my lymph nodes were some of the most blood vessel–rich nodes she'd ever seen; an ophthalmology appointment I had as a teenager when I was told that I had more blood vessels in my retinas than my doctor had ever seen; a benign polyp in my colon, identified at the beginning of medical school, that was engorged with blood vessels. This went way back. Even earlier than the blood moles, earlier than the liver cancer, earlier than everything. It also quickly became clear that VEGF could easily have contributed to the fluid that accumulated all over my body during each episode by opening up channels in blood vessels for fluid to pour out. Many of my symptoms were finally pointing back toward a common source.

The best thing about the emerging VEGF connection was that a drug already existed to block it specifically. This wouldn't be a shotgun fired in the dark; it would finally be a sniper shot. Blockers of VEGF were developed to treat cancer by shutting off the blood vessel growth the tumors needed, adding months to survival for patients with some of the worst cancers, like the form of brain cancer that my mom had (unfortunately, the VEGF blocker trial began enrollment just after her death). Yes, the possible adverse effects of the VEGF blocker were major, like uncontrolled bleeding and strokes, but . . . so were chemotherapy's. *Could this drug that was not developed enough in 2003 to help my mom end up helping me?*

Let me back up. The immune system works as a mind-bogglingly complex web of communication lines within cells and between cells through which cells speak to one another, keeping one another in a careful balance by indicating when each should come online, and when it should switch off. The complexity is fine-tuned—and when something goes wrong in one place, it can cascade, and the whole thing can fall apart. Quickly.

Many of the pieces of hardware that make up the cells composing the human body have been studied, named, categorized, and tested. That's not to say we know everything there is to know—not by a long shot—but we do have a good idea about how some things work normally and about how they work in disease states. Like so much else, a lot of this comes down to proteins.

Basically, every cell is a machine. Think about a computer. It comes programmed with a series of codes for it to perform a variety of functions. Every time the computer performs a function, such as calculating a math problem or making a sound, it relies on the series of codes that it was programmed with to execute the command. Similarly, the genetic code, which is a long sequence of about 3 billion nucleic acids that code for approximately twenty thousand different genes, is the instruction manual for making each protein that the cell could ever need to perform its functions. One marvel is how it all fits inside each microscopic cell. The DNA sequence in every single cell would stretch six feet long if fully unraveled, but it is wound up so tight into chromosomes that it fits into a space just 0.0002 inches across. And if the DNA sequences in *all* of just your cells were strung together, they would be about twice the diameter of the solar system.

The other marvel is how all of these individual machines with identical blueprints begin to differentiate, integrate and share information, and work together so seamlessly. Based on their particular cell types and demands on them at any given moment, cells use their genetic code to make specific proteins, which then perform the specific functions needed at that moment. Those functions may be to catalyze another protein to do something else, bind to another protein, or activate yet another. Biology is amazingly tangible, stepwise, and in no way magical. Think about your computer: It can't do anything that it doesn't have the software for or that it wasn't programmed to do.

But concrete biological rules become exponentially more complex when you consider that this hypothetical cell we're talking about is just one of billions of cells with myriad functions that must work together in a given organ and one of 37 trillion cells in the body. In fact, the signal for one cell (let's call it cell A) to use its genetic instruction map to make a particular protein often comes from another cell (let's call it cell B) that has secreted a protein, which has bound to cell A's receptor for that specific protein. The binding of the protein to cell A's receptor for that protein initiates a specific cascade of events within the cell that eventually reach the nucleus and signal for new proteins to be made. The cascade of events within the cell is kind of like a communication line or a game of dominoes. So, cells make and secrete proteins, which bind to receptors on other cells, initiating complex communication lines that instruct the receiving cells to make specific proteins. And on and on. Simultaneously throughout the body.

That's all settled science, but much of what we know about specific proteins and communication lines at the molecular level goes back barely two or three decades. That means that a huge source of knowledge is hardly older than your typical medical school graduate. There are still plenty of kinks to work out. Our limited ability to illuminate the exact nature of these pathways is perhaps matched by our limited ability to name them and their components elegantly. They're overly technical and require rote memorization of their origins of discovery, what drugs inhibit them, and so on. However, my adventures in pursuit of a cure for Castleman disease would reveal one example bursting with all of that information packed right into the name.

Back to the activated T cells and VEGF. Should we try the VEGF blocker? But what about the activated T cells? How did they fit together? Or was their relationship happenstance? It is known that activated T cells don't usually make VEGF. Did the activated T cells and the VEGF point back to a single source between them, or a way that they were in contact? I hated the idea of taking yet another new drug and risking attacking only one half of the iMCD equation with a VEGF blocker.

I considered the possibility of pairing the VEGF blocker with yet another chemotherapy carpet bomb, directed at my T cells, but I knew I'd be stacking up some truly horrific side effects. Maybe I could have withstood that kind of assault back before this all started, but I'd been weakened considerably by my many relapses. The chemo and VEGF blocker dual assault had to be reserved as my last resort.

Could there be some other factor, communication line, or cell type at play in both the T cell activation and increased VEGF? Something we hadn't yet seen, because we hadn't been looking for it?

I shook off my excitement and my fear and applied the last bit of focus I still had. I was in Philadelphia, Caitlin was with me, my family was behind me, my friends were supporting me . . . but it was up to me. It was overtime. Again. The fifth overtime. The ball was in my hands.

Then a cascade of memories of blood vessel growth, research articles, and medical school lectures came together. After years of study, diligence, desperate searching, and devastatingly false "aha!" moments.

Eureka!

Even though activated T cells don't make VEGF, the two *are* connected. I didn't have to discover it. It was already known that the same cellular line of communication needs to turn on for VEGF to be produced and for T cell activation to occur. It's called mammalian target of rapamycin, or mTOR for short.

Mammalian target of rapamycin is critical for immune cells that are ramping up for war to become activated, stay activated, and proliferate, and it is separately critical for cells to secrete VEGF. For both T cell activation and VEGF production, mTOR is the intermediary between the initiation signal the cell receives on its receptors and T cells going into activation mode and other cells making VEGF. You can think of it as a long, key stretch in a very miniature game of dominoes going on inside your cells. When the mTOR pathway gets activated, T cells will very soon be able to shift into fight mode, and many different cell types will be able to start making VEGF. Activation of mTOR is basically a green light for the immune system to mobilize. The war is on. For good or for ill.

It may seem like a simple connection that should have been landed on much sooner. But there are hundreds of other activators and downstream effects of the mTOR pathway. And hundreds of other pathways that overlap with the mTOR pathway. So you can think of that game of dominoes as actually being hundreds of games occurring simultaneously and intersecting in multiple dimensions using many of the same pieces. The T cell–VEGF-mTOR connection was not by any means clear-cut or certain to be the problem for me.

But it was something. I wondered: Could mTOR be overactive in me? Could that communication line be stuck in the on position, causing a civil war to be waged throughout my body despite there being no enemy in sight? More important, could targeting it and turning it off deactivate the T cells and shut off VEGF production? Could it stop this deadly and relentless disease? Researchers had already developed an mTOR inhibitor called sirolimus, which was approved by the FDA for patients

who received kidney transplants.* By blocking that communication line, sirolimus weakened cells of the immune system so that
they wouldn't attack and reject the newly transplanted organ. Of
course, that meant patients on sirolimus were susceptible to infections due to a weakened immune system, but sirolimus had a
much better side effect profile than the other two drugs I was
considering. It had never been used to treat anyone with iMCD.

Sirolimus is also known as rapamycin in homage to its discovery on the island of Rapa Nui. You might know Rapa Nui
as Easter Island or "that Pacific island with the giant stone figures." Rapamycin is a metabolite naturally produced by a bacte-
rium found in the soil of that island. A pharmaceutical company
called Ayerst had been collecting soil samples from islands all
over the Pacific in hopes of identifying antifungal agents when
they came across this compound on Rapa Nui, more than one
thousand miles from its nearest neighbor. Its distance from other
islands, the sheer number of islands that were visited, and the
many others that were not mean that it could have easily been
passed over. Then, there was an incredible convergence of science. Researchers had been trying to understand the function of
a recently discovered complex of proteins inside cells that would
later be named mammalian target of rapamycin. The name was
given after it was determined that rapamycin targeted and inhibited this protein complex. Finally, a name in biology that indicates what drug inhibits it and its origin of discovery!

But it still wasn't clear what mTOR actually did. Then, the
ability to inhibit this protein complex with rapamycin in laboratory experiments provided insights into how it worked and how
the drug worked too. Mammalian target of rapamycin was a
central hub for integrating diverse cellular signals and initiating

---

* It had also been studied in another rare disease called lymphangioleiomyomato-
sis. A mentor, colleague, and friend, Dr. Vera Krymskaya, actually made the key
discovery that led to the clinical trial of sirolimus and its FDA approval for that
disease.

various activities like cellular proliferation; the drug inhibited mTOR and thus stopped these activities. The symbiosis was beautiful. This rapid advancement of understanding revealed that sirolimus was a potent immunosuppressant and led to myriad clinical studies of its use. More recently, it has become clear that sirolimus actually extends lives of healthy mice, dogs, and other animals. The earlier in life that it's given, the longer these animals survive. This drug wasn't sounding too bad after all. The story of sirolimus was a triumph of ingenuity as well as investment. Those trips to remote Pacific islands, the stormy seas, the dirt samples, the giant stone figures keeping watch—that kind of perseverance and imagination is possible only in a project with big ambitions and long schedules. I was thrilled by the story and the promise it held for me.

Now I had a candidate immunosuppressant, which inhibited three new targets (mTOR, VEGF, and activated T cells) simultaneously, and I began to think about treating myself with it to see if it could stop my immune system from spiraling out of control and thus prevent relapses. But yet again, this treatment approach didn't make any sense under the previous way of thinking about iMCD. Traditionalists would certainly have wondered why I wanted to suppress immune activity. This was a lymph node disorder, they'd say. It was excessive IL-6. I just needed to block IL-6 and ablate the lymph node with more chemo.

Ah, but the traditionalists had ignored those blood moles too.

Before anything else, I knew I needed to test the levels of mTOR activation in my tissue. I pulled out the stored lymph node tissue that had been resected a few weeks before and performed a study to measure the levels of a protein called phospho-S6. Phospho-S6 increases when mTOR is active. It came back strongly increased. Mammalian target of rapamycin *was* active. This still didn't mean that blocking it would be an effective treatment. There's no blood test or known examination that would give us that information. There were likely lots of other communication lines also turned on. And we didn't know why mTOR activation was increased. But the T cell–VEGF-mTOR connection was starting to feel like a bit more than a hunch. That was more than anything else. And it was enough. Time to go.

There wasn't time to set up a formal clinical trial, and we likely didn't have enough data to support one then anyway. I don't think I would have felt comfortable trying the treatment on another patient based on our limited data; there were too many unknowns. Would it work? Plus, who knew what problems could arise when you shut down one part of a volatile immune system like mine? Maybe it would actually trigger a relapse?

I traveled down to the National Institutes of Health to speak with Dr. Tom Uldrick, a member of the CDCN Scientific Advisory Board, who had always impressed me with his data-driven approach to medicine and his focus on his patients. Not just focus, he advocated for and championed his patients' needs. He was exactly whom I needed to talk to. Our bald heads (he pulls off the bald head much better than I do) glistened in the light-filled atrium of the institute's Magnuson Clinical Center as we reviewed the data. The brochure for the center states "patients, the Clinical Center's partners in discovery." This could not have been more true than it was that day. Our meeting location was significant too. The atrium is famous for casual exchange of scientific ideas leading to medical breakthroughs that have occurred at the NIH. It literally sits between the NIH's buildings dedicated to basic science research, clinical research, and patient care. Tom and I were at a similar intersection of research and patient care. We agreed, especially in the absence of other options, that treating with an mTOR inhibitor made sense. We considered newer versions of drugs similar to sirolimus, but Tom noted that sirolimus had almost twenty-five years of safety data behind it, and he was aware of it inducing regression of a particular type of tumor with increased blood vessel growth similar to my lymph nodes.* It just hadn't been used to treat iMCD. Yet.

There has to be a first for everything.

Or, put another way: The fact that it hasn't been tried yet doesn't mean it won't work.

Or the fact that it's your first or second delivery doesn't mean the baby won't be delivered safely.

The T cell–VEGF-mTOR connection was our strongest hunch among a seemingly infinite number of alternative ideas. Maybe some of those options would be better. We needed more data to know. But time was running out and we had to begin testing something empirically. I felt strongly that I couldn't let a lack of data prevent this first use. I had to be the guinea pig.

Dr. van Rhee gave his blessing, and so in February 2014 I started testing sirolimus on the nearest subject I could find: myself. I decided to keep those monthly infusions of IVIg going too; it had done *something* during that last relapse, and I wasn't ready to stop it just yet.

Again, I was scared. I did notice improvement in several of my symptoms almost immediately after starting the sirolimus, but since most of my blood tests had already normalized, I couldn't get any objective indication if it was working until my time between relapses was extended. At that point, I'd been averaging a relapse approximately every nine months. All I could do was track my symptoms and lab tests while I waited. Then I got just the boost of confidence that I needed. The *Blood* journal editors emailed Chris, Frits, and me to say that they would accept our paper with only a few minor edits. It was exhilarating to know that our work would be published and disseminated so

---

* In patients who developed Kaposi sarcoma after kidney transplantation, changing from cyclosporine to sirolimus allowed for continued immune regulation and regression of the blood vessel–rich Kaposi sarcoma tumors.

broadly. For me personally, it was an important lesson: *Never stop questioning and always follow the data.* We might be on the right path about this disease being about immune system function above all else. And therefore maybe sirolimus would work. Only time would tell. I really just wanted to make it to May, because Caitlin and I had finally mustered up the confidence to place our save-the-date postcards and then the wedding invitations in the mail. There was no turning back.

CHAPTER SIXTEEN

THERE WERE TWO big questions as May 24 approached.

Question One: Was the sirolimus treatment going to hold? I had doubts. These doubts were well-founded (if anything, my experiences over the past few years had given me an education in skepticism). As I said earlier—I'm an empiricist, and I knew better than to be fooled by one study, especially one of only a few weeks in a single patient (me). I understood all too well that breakthroughs can take years and there are twists and turns that no one can expect. The last few weeks had been some of the happiest of my life—I'd even taken that road trip with my closest friends to the Grand Canyon that Ben and I had mused about during my first hospitalization. Ben and I also celebrated the news that he and his wife were expecting their first child and wanted me to be his godfather; but that didn't mean these moments would last.

Question Two: Was I going to have any hair at my wedding? It's not lost on me that the length of my hair should have been the least of my worries. But this second question occupied at least as much of my thoughts as the first one. I'm pretty sure Caitlin thought about it too, although she was politely quiet on the issue.

It wasn't vanity. I just wanted Caitlin to see Dave on our wedding day. She had so selflessly been with David Fajgenbaum, the patient, for so long. My baldness was a clear reminder of what I had just been through and what still simmered beneath the surface for me. I wanted to give her Dave. The Dave she had first fallen in love with (though with a lot less muscle than before), and the one I hoped she'd have for a very long time to come.

Dave, who just happened to have really, really short hair.

Of course, with hair growth I couldn't take matters into my own hands, as I'd been doing and preaching about for medical research. In this one instance, Santa Claus was just going to have to deliver—I would sit and wait and hope. Every once in a while, that happens to work.

With only days to spare, my hair started to grow back. On the day of the wedding, my groomsmen gathered in my hotel room to get ready. Grant was shaving next to me and offered to trim some of the hair that had grown on the back of my neck. I declined—every hair counted! It *almost* looked like I had a (severe) buzz cut when Caitlin and I walked down the aisle.

May 24 was such a happy day. Our joy that it was finally happening was amplified by memories of when it almost never could have. It felt like we had all collectively walked through the one and only door in a long hallway that led to happiness. I couldn't stop smiling the whole day. I was marrying the girl of my dreams—a woman who had recently been packing my body with ice like I was a coho salmon at Whole Foods. Here she was saying "in sickness and in health, until death do us part" and I didn't have to guess that she really meant it; I knew she'd be there for me. She had the "in sickness" part down, so I figured the "in health" part would be in the bag too.

Back when I was semiconscious, back in between the loud beeps of machines in the ICU, I had dreamed of getting to marry Caitlin even if it was the last thing I did before I died. But when the day finally arrived, I didn't feel that desperation; I felt simply as though we were finally beginning the life we'd wanted to start earlier, and that we had so much more to do together.

Almost everything about our wedding day was perfect. I was responsible for one misstep during the ceremony. I'm not sure *what* made me think it was time to go in for the kiss when I did, but right after we exchanged rings, I thought it, so, you know, I did it . . . and Caitlin had to stiff-arm me before I could get within range. Our guests burst out laughing. The priest laughed too and said, "Not yet, there will be time for that." I guess I wasn't used to the idea that I had time, lots of time, to do what I wanted. It was a feeling I was eager to relearn.

My dad was responsible for another um . . . moment. The ceremony had ended and the dancing had commenced—and then the music suddenly stopped. I looked onstage and saw what I had been quietly fearing: My dad had taken the guitar from the band. Ever the entertainer, he was known to take the stage at events like this. We had even warned the band that he might try this. They had assured me they'd keep it away from him, that never in twenty-five years of weddings had they permitted a guest to play. I don't know what he said (or how much of a tip he slipped them), but there he was, guitar in hand, beaming with satisfaction.

I knew what that meant. My father is not a sentimental man. He wasn't going to play a love song. To put it politely, he has a colorful sense of humor. The saving grace was the thickness of his Caribbean accent. Except for the twenty-four Trinidadians in attendance, none of the guests could make out the inappropriate lyrics of the songs he sang. I was about ready to jump up and start pulling plugs, but I stopped myself. We were in a ballroom that was just about a mile down the road from the ICU in

Philadelphia where my dad and I had shared a room when I first became sick. I remembered him staying with me, pestering doctors, keeping notes, calling in favors . . . and he never left my side for relapse after relapse after relapse after relapse. I realized that he deserved this. I wasn't the only one who'd been through the wringer. My family had too. I was getting married; my dad deserved his moment in the spotlight. And, right on cue, he used that moment to sing the songs about the "man with the big bamboo" and the "honeymoonin' couple" who were fighting about who should be "on top" (of the suitcase they were trying to close). At least my Trini relatives were laughing.

In the lead-up to the wedding, I had not taken my foot off the proverbial gas on my Castleman disease research. I wasn't going to make the mistake of throttling down because I'd found a treatment that might be promising. After the wedding, though, the CDCN team really started to take shape. I began to recruit colleagues in earnest, and for the first time I was including my story as part of the CDCN story. I was breaking my silence as a patient with the disease that, before, I had been presenting as solely a professional interest.

It may sound minor, but this shift felt momentous. I started to talk in public about my diagnosis and what I'd been through. I went back to business school in the fall, and I no longer tried to hide my health from my classmates and colleagues. No more secrets. It was no longer important to me to present myself as two different people—the "serious" physician-scientist–MBA student who went to school, studied medicine, led the CDCN, and conducted research, and the sick me. I was both things at once, and from that point on, I knew I always would be.

My newfound openness engendered many offers of help, which I gladly accepted. I started to assemble a sort of Castleman commando team—the kind you see in movies, made up of a surprisingly motley and complementary group of people.

The main difference between us and real commandos, however, was that we had no money. Castleman disease isn't just incurable, it's underfunded. Business school made me realize that I had neglected this side of the equation, and it was severely limiting our potential. Our organization couldn't just be a few medical school friends, patients, and loved ones working on nights and weekends with an annual budget of $15,000. Other diseases with similar incidence, like ALS and cystic fibrosis, had multiple orders of magnitude more research funding: More than $50 million of public and private funds go toward ALS research every year; $80 million for cystic fibrosis. And those diseases deserve and need more too! If it hadn't been clear to me before, it was now: We couldn't do it on our own, not at one-fiftieth of 1 percent of the funding for similar rare diseases. If we really wanted to turn the tide against Castleman disease, we needed to expand our effort to include more than just those directly affected by it. More people needed to learn about it, so it wouldn't continue to be one of the most deadly, most common diseases that most people have never heard of. We needed to start a movement to raise more funds for our research from the general public, and we needed more manpower to execute our ambitious research agenda.

One of the first commandos was a business school classmate named Steven Hendricks, a six-foot-seven former NASA engineer and a wizard at turning our esoteric medical jargon into public-ready words that told our story and broadened our reach. He took on our website relaunch and built a new online patient community. He was also excellent at telling me I was wrong. I needed that. My background still made me research-oriented— I always wanted to go over results, find new leads, and pursue those leads above all else—but Steven would tell me, "No, Dave, it can't all be about the research." He was right. Medicine in the twenty-first century isn't a separate, celestial pursuit, carried out in laboratories and libraries. Medicine isn't just science; it's advocacy too. The possibility of healing depends on the ability of men and women to marshal efforts toward that healing. It depends on money, and it depends on storytelling. Steven helped me realize that. He also loved to make the point that biomedical research was just *begging* to be revolutionized and accelerated with nascent technologies and disruptive approaches, just as so many other industries had been in the past few years. He would go on to say that our approach to transforming biomedical research for Castleman disease "wasn't rocket science" and our repeatable steps needed to be spread to other diseases. He was the only person I'd ever met who could actually compare things to rocket science and know exactly what he was talking about.

Another business school classmate, Sean Craig, who was a former Army officer, West Point grad, and project manager at Exxon, came into the CDCN with one mission: to infuse order and structure. He built new planning documents to track our progress virtually and to strengthen our organizational infrastructure; he effectively split our volunteer team members into multiple divisions. He was exactly what our rabble needed. And almost best of all, despite his Beast-like exterior and pedigree, he too shared an appreciation for Borat. Game recognizes game.

Barclay Nihill, a business school classmate and former private equity investor, would evaluate our projects in terms of "investments"—of time, talent, and treasure—and pushed us to work in ways that could be quantitatively measured. He wanted us to be able to convince numbers wonks like him of our value and impact. He was also classically scrappy—physically one of the smallest among us, but he would have done anything for our team.

Sheila Pierson, a four-foot-ten graduate student studying medical informatics, shared Barclay's scrappiness and stature.

Despite her tininess, she was a magician with big data analytics. And her innate gravitational pull to help those in need meant that she worked long hours to turn simple numbers into meaningful insights that could save patients' lives.

Dustin Shilling, who had just completed his PhD in neuroscience, instilled a healthy skepticism of so-called breakthroughs. As an Alzheimer's researcher, he had learned all too well about the importance of the scientific method and interrogating results before getting too excited. He pushed for, and contributed his time toward, developing large-scale studies with meticulously detailed designs. The kinds of studies that could stand up in a field as complicated as Alzheimer's or Castleman disease.

Jason Ruth, a PhD student studying cancer biology, was my friend before he was my colleague. After joining our clan, he quickly revealed one of his superpowers: He could make connections in his mind between seemingly disparate ideas. *That new observation in Castleman disease? There was a cancer research study published in 2005 that could help to explain its importance. Those elevated molecules? Have you seen what other diseases they are elevated in?* Biology is intricate and interwoven across species and diseases. Jason made use of all of it to inform whatever problem he was trying to solve. It was sort of like a mountain climber between two faces who uses footholds and handgrips on one to get his way up the other. I envied that kind of thinking—my hyperfocus kept me running straight forward more often than not.

It wasn't just Penn graduate students on our commando team. Some of the most important members were already with me. My mother-in-law, Patty, father-in-law, Bernie, and Caitlin also took up the call to arms. Patty became the CDCN's community coordinator, serving as the primary point of contact for patients, loved ones, and our growing leadership team. She was perfect for it, comforting patients and encouraging volunteers. Bernie became the first member of and a linchpin for an advisory council of leaders in business, law, and medicine who help to guide the CDCN. Caitlin led our communications efforts, helped with event coordination, and provided daily counsel and candid advice to me. One of Caitlin's best friends came on board too. Mary Zuccato, an MBA student simultaneously climbing the leadership ladder at Vanguard, managed to jump-start and expand our fundraising efforts; as of my writing this page, we're finally at about 1 percent of the annual funding for similar rare diseases. Mary became our chief operating officer, which she did as a volunteer on top of her full-time finance work. She was perfect for the role: I've never met anyone who more intuitively and gracefully turns ideas into action. She's a *machine* for action. Just being around her is motivational.

Soon, people outside of Penn and my family began to offer to help too. The CDCN leadership team expanded to include other patients, loved ones, physicians, and students—all of us volunteers, each giving anywhere from three to thirty hours each week to the mission: cure Castleman disease. While the hours our CDCN volunteers gave were necessary for our success, it has been their diverse backgrounds and the network's unique approach that have led to innovative solutions and our accelerated pace of progress. A lot had changed since the days when our "team" consisted of my dad, my sisters, and Caitlin, gathered around a hospital bed, chasing paperwork and cold-calling experts with a mission to just keep me alive. We had scale now—and momentum.

One person who helped to begin turning our momentum into impact was Raj Jayanthan. Raj became ill with iMCD during his third year of medical school and, like me, had near-fatal organ failure. Just like for me and so many other iMCD patients, doctors at a top-tier medical system couldn't do anything to slow his disease down. It wasn't until Dr. Uldrick from the NIH was consulted and recommended a different treatment approach, involving combination chemotherapy, that Raj began to improve. Tom thought connecting Raj and me by email would be a good idea given our shared journeys.

Our first phone call—three hours long—was just eleven days after Raj was discharged from that frightening hospitalization and I was between my fourth and fifth flares. We immediately bonded over our shared nightmare. We recounted the intimate and eerily similar details of our experiences—we'd both noticed those peculiar blood moles growing rapidly just before becoming sick and we'd both had the surreal feeling of being patients just weeks after walking the same hospital hallways as medical students. Though our symptoms and clinical journeys were almost identical, we had responded *completely* differently to various treatments. This was an important reminder to me that nothing about Castleman disease was straightforward and that I couldn't be lulled into thinking that what worked for me would necessarily work for everyone (or anyone) else.

I was the first Castleman disease patient that Raj had spoken to. I knew what it meant to him, because I still remembered the first patient I met, in Dr. van Rhee's waiting room years before. But our call also meant so much to me, because it was clear that Raj wanted to help the cause however he could. At the end of our conversation, he asked me to send him the best research papers on Castleman disease, so he could get up to speed.

My relapse shortly thereafter, in 2013, galvanized Raj's decision to join the fight. After hearing how sick I got with my fifth episode and remembering how sick he had been himself, Raj took six months off from medical school to dedicate 100 percent of his effort to the most important aspect of the CDCN's fight at that time: systematically collecting clinical, research, and treatment data in a central database for analysis.

Recognizing that sirolimus, the drug I was taking for iMCD, had the potential to make a huge difference in my life and possibly the lives of others, we wondered about how many other drugs might already be approved for something else that could help iMCD patients right away. This practice of "off-label" drug use is common, but information on what diseases these drugs are tried on and whether they worked is almost never tracked by the medical system to guide future use. In fact, medical records systems almost never have a specific data field to record whether a treatment is working. And even if they did, physicians and researchers can see medical data only on patients at their own institutions. Disease registries and natural history studies attempt to collect these data for some diseases, but major issues with such studies limit the usefulness of the data. We needed to do better.*

We needed to create a study to systematically track the various treatments used in Castleman disease and their effectiveness across a large patient population while also collecting as much clinical and laboratory data as possible to start to solve some of the other mysteries of Castleman disease (really this should be done for all diseases). Raj enthusiastically agreed to assist with building the foundation of a Castleman disease registry study to accomplish this. But there was precious little precedent for how to do this well. Like so much else in medicine, there were deep, arbitrary divisions between groups supposedly oriented toward the same goal of curing disease.

To determine our approach, we evaluated over twenty other disease registries and laid out the pros and cons of each. Some registries were patient-powered, which meant that patients enrolled online and entered data themselves. These registries had the highest patient enrollment numbers, because participants

---

* Before we tried to build a registry study, we decided the best option for generating insights in the short term was to conduct a study that analyzed data on the treatments given to iMCD patients in previously published case reports. We learned of a lot of drugs that had been tried, but the data on how effective they were were inherently biased. Case reports are typically published only when a relatively novel treatment works (unfortunately, physicians and researchers often don't publish when things don't work), so our study likely highlighted the exceptions more often than the rules.

could be recruited online, but they had relatively weaker medical data quality and richness because they relied on a patient's *memory* for all data entered, even lab test results, sometimes from hospitalizations years before.

On the other hand, physician-powered registries involved physicians at a few select sites enrolling patients and entering medical data on them. These registries are more expensive and traditionally have lower patient enrollment, because they're limited to patients treated at those select sites, but they have much stronger medical data quality and depth. However, the pace of data entry is significantly limited by how busy physicians are with other responsibilities.

We wanted to figure out a way to combine the best aspects of both approaches into a hybrid model. After months of review and drafting, the plan finally coalesced, fittingly, in the NIH's clinical center atrium. Tom, Grant, Raj, and I were huddled around a table not far from the one where Tom and I had earlier discussed the possibility of using sirolimus to treat me. Our registry study would be patient-powered, so patients would enroll themselves directly online from anywhere in the world. But rather than rely on patients to enter all their data, we would get permission from them to obtain their complete medical records from their physicians. Then, trained data analysts would enter extensive, physician-quality data from those records into the registry. We'd get the best of both worlds: high patient enrollment and high data quality. And it would happen quickly, because neither patients nor physicians would be burdened with data entry.

Over several months, we worked with patients and hospitals to figure out how to execute this first-of-its-kind registry study. Frankly, it was astonishing to see so clearly how obstacles to accessing data are such a big part of the dysfunction in medicine. More often than not, the data are out there, ready to be collected, and willingly given up by patients and sometimes by

hospital systems. Getting past these hurdles took the will to ignore the status quo and to keep pushing. Raj had that will. I did
too. It helped that we both have the disease we hoped this effort
would cure.

But we still needed funding; for starters, it would take a lot of
money to hire those expert data analysts. It was time to try to
partner with pharma for help. After multiple exploratory calls
with officials from a large pharmaceutical company, we had them
interested. We were asked to set up a meeting with executives
from their North American offices and to teleconference in executives from their European offices. This was a huge opportunity, and we hoped to demonstrate that we weren't just a group
of young patients and physician-scientists in training but that we
had an idea worth their support. So we worked on our proposal,
and worked some more . . . and more . . . and perfected the
pitch, and made the slickest presentation possible . . . After our
umpteenth rehearsal, our small team of graduate and (barely)
postgraduate, mid-to-late-twentysomethings walked into the
room just in time for the start of the meeting, only to discover
that the conference room didn't have a working telephone line.
None of us could believe it, and despite the collective years of
education assembled there, the technicalities of conference calling were lost on us. Suddenly it was four minutes past the scheduled time. Then it was five minutes past. Everybody was either
scrambling for a solution or frozen in panic.

Eventually we went low-tech: We called the teleconference
number from my iPhone and then passed it around the room so
that each of us could make our portion of the presentation directly into the mouthpiece. I was so frazzled I forgot to mention
that I was the executive director of the CDCN or that I was a
newly appointed adjunct faculty member in the University of
Pennsylvania medical school. I mentioned only that I was an
MBA student. But even if we fumbled to make the call work,
Raj and I were on a mission, and I suspect that our drive cov-

ered up our mistakes that day. If we'd been trying to sell widgets, we would have crashed and burned. But we had a fire burning inside of us for a cause whose success our lives literally depended on, and everyone in that meeting could feel it. And in the end— after another high-stakes meeting at their offices with senior management—they agreed to partner with the CDCN and University of Pennsylvania to establish our international registry study. Raj had already gone back to medical school by that subsequent meeting, but Jason Ruth and Arthur Rubenstein had joined me. The three of us struggled to contain our excitement as we hurried out of the room and through the building. But once we were outside, it all came out—we jumped up and down and cheered (while the pharmaceutical executives were probably watching from their windows!).

On the two-hour car ride back to Philadelphia, I asked Jason if he could join Caitlin and me for dinner to celebrate. He demurred, explaining that he had to go home to prepare for his PhD thesis defense, which was the next day. I almost drove off the road. Jason had possibly the most important day of his career coming up, when he'd be giving a presentation about the last five years of his laboratory research! But he didn't want to let me know any sooner, because he wanted to help, even if it meant putting his final defense preparation on hold. Not surprisingly, he passed with flying colors and was recruited to do a postdoctoral fellowship in one of the top cancer research laboratories in the world, at the Broad Institute of MIT and Harvard. As of this writing, he works in biotech venture capital investing and continues to help lead the CDCN as volunteer chief scientific officer.

January 5, 2015, marked one year since my last relapse ended and my fifth overtime began. But I was cautious. I had been here before—indeed, I'd tentatively celebrated one-year remissions twice before—and remembered all too well that I relapsed soon thereafter.

As I approached the sixteen-month mark—the longest I'd ever gone between relapses—I started to feel some low-grade flu-like symptoms. Caitlin became so worried that she took a leave from her job to maximize her time with me and give us the flexibility to travel together for vacation . . . or go to Little Rock on short notice. But my blood test results kept looking great. Those inflammatory markers I'd found during the fifth episode, showing elevated VEGF and T cell activation, remained normal. I just had the flu. No one has ever been more excited or relieved to have the flu. After a short break, Caitlin felt comfortable returning to work.

And then, one day, I crossed that dreaded sixteen-month threshold. I was in uncharted territory. I felt like I had been in some disaster movie, holed up in my bunker, and I'd finally emerged, blinking into the brightness of the sun. The meteor hadn't struck after all—Will Smith had saved the day. Or sirolimus, in my case. But I knew this still didn't mean that my disease would never be back. Those movies almost always have sequels.

CHAPTER SEVENTEEN

"YOU'RE GOING TO die in this role."

This assessment came from a new colleague who thought I was in way over my head when I accepted an offer to join the full-time faculty as an assistant professor of medicine at the University of Pennsylvania after graduating from Wharton. I think he meant it idiomatically or must not have known that I had a terminal illness. But part of me had to laugh, privately, at his faux pas. I had important work to push forward and was very much planning not to die in my new role. I would be happy to prove him wrong.

In my new position, I would be able to focus almost entirely on conducting and coordinating research to cure Castleman disease and solve mysteries of the immune system. And all from the place where this awful and awe-inspiring journey had started. I would create and direct a research program that would include both what we call a wet bench lab—a laboratory set up to work with patient tissues, cell lines, model systems, and other biological material—and a computational lab, focused primarily on

big data analytics. In scientific terms, this is translational research: We translate what we learn from in-depth clinical data
analyses to guide which lab experiments to perform on patient
biospecimens; we translate those findings back to the clinical
research arena for further testing; and then, we try to translate it
all into new drugs or diagnostic tools for patients.

In my new faculty role, I also codirected a one-week course
to teach fourth-year medical students about precision medicine
and, indirectly, how to think outside the box (without needing
to nearly die five times first). Precision medicine, or personal-
ized medicine as it's sometimes called, is a new approach to
disease management whereby each patient is treated based on
her or his precise genetic makeup and specific disease character-
istics, rather than treating everyone with a particular disease in
the same way. Using sirolimus, which is typically prescribed to
kidney transplant patients, to treat me, an iMCD patient, based
on results from studies done on my samples, is an example of
precision medicine in action. I'm a walking, talking advertise-
ment for its value.

I also took on an official role in the Orphan Disease Center,
combining everything I had learned from my CDCN commando team to help accelerate rare disease research. And I continued to lead the CDCN as volunteer executive director. I'd
been dreaming of doing this kind of work since I was eighteen,
when my mom first got sick. It was often thrilling. And it was
sometimes horrible.

My new office would be in the same hospital building where
I first became so ill and in which I nearly died. It was . . . un-
pleasant initially. I ticked the boxes on a few PTSD symptoms
every time I walked through those doors, for sure. But I was
determined to replace my memories from weeks of agony with
positive memories of making progress against Castleman disease.

One of the first of these memories came quite suddenly. One
day in March 2016, I got multiple emails and phone calls within

minutes. There was a newly diagnosed iMCD patient in the ICU: a military veteran in his mid-forties named Gary. As it happened, I'd managed to avoid the ICU as a patient for a couple of years and as a physician-scientist for even longer. First unconsciously, and then quite consciously indeed. I guess I just needed some space from the place. We'd been intimate for a long time and the relationship had been rocky. Off and on; on and off.

But no more. I needed to see how I could help this patient and then find out if he was interested in joining one of our studies. I got his room number and took the elevator up a couple floors from my office. Gary's wife was standing against the window when I came in—and something in the view beyond her looked familiar, though I couldn't pinpoint what it was.

I was immediately struck by how sick Gary was—filled with fluid, tubes and probes all over his body, a dialysis machine continuously doing the work of his failing kidneys, two units of blood transfusing into his veins, and a ventilator that he had just been weaned off of still in the room—*and* how much he looked like I did when I was at my sickest. His wife's eyes radiated pain, and I recognized that too.

I explained my research and the work of the CDCN. They had heard of it already and were glad to be able to have a direct connection to it. "We are going to beat this disease," I said.

The look in their eyes began to change. I could tell that they were also both surprised. They told me that they had expected someone much older, who, according to them, was "detached, ailing, and preferred to be hidden away behind a microscope." Seeing me walk into the room, looking completely healthy, gave them hope that he could get out of there.

I told Gary about a study that I was running and how his blood samples could be helpful for better understanding this disease. It's rare to be able to get patient samples before major treatments have been administered, so these samples would be quite precious. He agreed to provide blood samples for the study—he seemed to be thrilled by the idea that he could be of material assistance. He was unable to lift his hand off the bed because of his full-body weakness, so we placed the necessary paperwork under his hand for a scribbled signature to memorialize his consent.

"We are going to beat this disease," I repeated. Gary later told me that the *we* was important. Just like me, Gary had felt as if iMCD had singled him out and he was on his own. Now he felt like he was part of something bigger than himself. I could relate.

As I walked out of the room, I saw Ashlee, who had been my own nurse for much of my stay in this same ICU. I hadn't seen her since. "David, is that you? Wow, you look great. You know that was your room, right?" Now I knew why that view had caught my attention. I don't remember too much from that first hospitalization, but I had stared out that window dreaming of what could be if I would survive. Here I was right back where it all started.

A lot had changed since then. It had taken *months* for me to be diagnosed; Gary was diagnosed within two days of arriving. That didn't happen by chance. Or by mere hope.

Six months prior, in a building across the street from Gary's ICU room, I had chaired a CDCN meeting of the top thirty-four iMCD experts from eight countries on five continents to establish the diagnostic criteria for iMCD. Amazingly, up to that point there was no agreed-upon checklist for physicians to determine if a patient had iMCD. Nearly every disease had one of these checklists, but not iMCD or any of the other subtypes of Castleman disease. It had taken about two years to aggregate the data and biospecimens from 244 patients, which we used to develop the diagnostic criteria. The meeting went close to how you'd expect a meeting of thirty-four international experts to go. Everyone had an opinion about what the criteria should include. There were a lot of disagreements. Some over substance, others over misinterpretation due to language barriers. But we kept coming back to the data, which helped us to eventually agree on the first-ever diagnostic criteria for iMCD. Our work was subsequently published in the journal *Blood*.

More than sixty years had passed since Benjamin Castleman's first published paper about the disease. Now physicians finally had a checklist to use when considering a diagnosis of iMCD, a map and instructions for how to get to their destination.

This was a huge win. You can't treat or save a single patient's life if you can't properly diagnose the disease. Another problem with not having diagnostic criteria is that incorrectly diagnosing people when they don't have Castleman disease sets back research and drug development, because these patients skew the results of studies. As expected, the new criteria have greatly sped up the time to diagnosis for patients and systematized their identification for research.

And I could see the results of that work right in front of me. Gary's doctors recommended performing a lymph node biopsy based on the new criteria. The pathologist who reviewed his biopsy was a key contributing author of that very paper. In fact, she and I had reviewed lymph node tissue from more than one hundred iMCD patients as part of the project. So when she looked at Gary's lymph node that day, she knew immediately that it was iMCD, and she had a checklist of criteria to prove it.

Most important, Gary's rapid diagnosis meant that he got a dose of siltuximab—which had been approved by the FDA for iMCD in 2014—right away and slowly improved. There really had been a sea change in treatment since I had first become ill, in 2010.

As Gary continued to improve, he provided repeated blood samples, and we were able to run experiments in real time. We were surprised by the changes we were observing: His T cells were even *more* highly activated and out of control than mine had been. The implication was obvious and scary: His was a serious case. I remembered how terrible my symptoms had been, and it seemed like he was suffering even more. But finally, after being hospitalized for two months, he was discharged to a rehab facility, where he would have to learn to walk again. We needed to continue to analyze samples, and I liked visiting with him, so I regularly drove to get vials of blood from him. When I told him that I'd keep the vials of blood in my chest pocket to keep them warm for the drive back to Philadelphia, he said I was just like a mother hen. His comment sparked an idea: Maybe I *should* just sit on them for the ride back. The plastic tubes were virtually unbreakable. And—*think it, do it!* (We've subsequently discontinued the "mother hen" mode of transportation since we determined that I'd need to sit on every sample we received to ensure identical experimental conditions. It was an easy decision.)

Gary's case felt like such a triumph. He was alive because of two major accomplishments that the CDCN, Dr. van Rhee, and I had played major parts in: the diagnostic criteria now being used worldwide to diagnose iMCD and the FDA's approval of siltuximab. I saw the impact of this work firsthand only because it happened a couple of floors above my office. Though I got lots of emails from physicians and patients, I still wondered about how many thousands of other patients around the world were benefiting from our work that I didn't know about. It was an awesome feeling. Even more, the data from Gary's samples would lead to new insights that could save other patients' lives too.

But a month later, Castleman disease pulled me back down to reality. Gary relapsed while on siltuximab. Nothing worked. Carpet bombing was commenced of cytotoxic chemotherapies that I was all too familiar with. But he didn't even respond to those. When his ICU nurse overheard me saying to his wife that there was still hope and that Gary could still pull through, she pulled me aside to say, in fact, there was no way he'd make it through the night and I needed to temper my optimism.

I hugged Caitlin a little longer than usual and spent more time on the phone with my family that night. I could finally understand how scared and helpless this disease makes those we love. Amazingly, however, the chemo kicked in just in time and Gary began to improve. He eventually walked out of the hospital and has been relapse-free for the last two years. It's always better not to anthropomorphize illness, especially as a doctor, but I've grown to hate the chaotic nature of iMCD as much as anything. Its brutality at least is knowable, and we've been able to glean evidence of its inner workings from its aggression. But as it did many times with me, when it seems to arbitrarily "choose" to relent in the face of some treatments but not others—and to storm back unexpectedly—it highlights just how little we know.

And sometimes I despaired that we could never learn fast enough. Elyse was a twelve-year-old girl from Boston and typical for her age in many ways: quiet and anxious around big groups, but totally comfortable around her family and friends. She loved to bake cakes and cookies and even dreamed of having her own bakery one day. But then she started having unexplained abdominal pain and skin rashes. Frequent ER visits didn't lead to any answers. Then, just three days after her thirteenth birthday, she told her mom that she was feeling "off," a feeling that escalated enough to get her admitted to the hospital and then the ICU. When her doctors finally diagnosed Castleman disease, Elyse and her mom went through many of the same things that my dad and I had gone through three years before. Her mom, Kim, googled Castleman disease; the results weren't helpful. Elyse asked the doctor if she was going to be okay. "Well, not much is known about this disease, but it's not lymphoma or another type of cancer, so we hope so." Kim grabbed on to that hope with everything she had. Kim never left Elyse's side. Elyse spent the next eight months battling Castleman disease, mostly in the ICU, but nothing could stop it. It was relentless.

Elyse passed away despite months of her physicians' best attempts to apply the best tools available. It wasn't that she was at the wrong hospital, that they didn't have enough time, or that someone else could have done something differently. Nothing more could have been done even based on what we know today. Sadly, Elyse's story happens all too often. She was truly special, and you can see that in the legacy she has left through her family and friends, but what happened to her is not unique. I look at her picture on the wall in my office every day—she would have turned eighteen this year and would probably have baked her signature tie-dye-frosted cupcakes. Her picture—among those of other patients who have died and those who are still fighting—reminds me that we've just scratched the surface with our understanding of Castleman disease.

Every patient who dies battling Castleman disease and every biospecimen removed during a patient's battle harbors microscopic clues into the mysteries of this beastly disease, how the immune system works, and how it may be manipulated to treat Castleman disease and potentially other illnesses too. Simply put, the cure for this disease is within each of us. It's just waiting to be pieced together. Therefore, we collect medical data and samples from deceased patients as a final legacy to try to harness the clues they leave so we can better help future patients.

It's not just Elyse's samples and data that continue to be a lasting legacy in this fight against Castleman disease. Kim now serves on the board of the CDCN, and she leads a motorcycle ride fundraiser every year. The ride memorializes Elyse's life and raises money to help find treatments and a cure for other young people with Castleman disease. Kim is creating silver linings every day, and the rest of us are in her debt for it.

CHAPTER EIGHTEEN

THE LEGEND OF the Faustian bargain goes like this: Faust was a doctor who wasn't satisfied with what he knew (which was a lot). So he made a deal with the devil: He would gain all of the knowledge in the world, and all the power and pleasure that comes with it, but he would have to give up his soul. It was a pretty good bargain—right until he was dragged down to hell by a bunch of demons come to collect.

Before I got Castleman disease, I was well on my way to an education and career that promised close to supreme authority. We live in a mostly secular, individualistic age, but can you tell me there's nothing sacred about the symbols of medicine? The white coat and the staff of Asclepius, the waiting room and the inner chambers, the pronouncements, the scribbled commandments. I was ready to join that priestly class and tap into the knowledge of the ages. I would be an instrument of life and death.

And then my own life got very tenuous, almost hell-like. So I did what I was supposed to do: I appealed to the authority and supremacy of medicine. I got the wrong answer back. I appealed again. I got the wrong answer back. I didn't die, but that was providence.

Then I stopped believing in an omniscient medical system.

I pulled a reverse Faust.

I rejected the belief that any institution had all the answers or represented all the available knowledge in the world. I stopped hoping for the solutions. Instead of appealing to the magical and mysterious power of a higher authority to gain knowledge, I read books, reviewed studies, and investigated proteins. There was work to be done.

I made it through several more terrible episodes of illness— and then something like a reprieve. I'm realistic about it. That's what I have now. A reprieve.

But there's another aspect to the reverse Faustian bargain. I had started out trying to save my own life. Now I'm working to save so many others. It feels like my soul has stretched its borders, and it has come into contact with others' in a way I could never have anticipated. This wasn't short-term gain in exchange for long-term consequences, like Faust's. In return for giving up the possibility of omniscience and enduring a living hell, I got a larger life, one more connected to others, and a shared sense of responsibility. I got more than I even could have imagined. And often still less than I have wanted.

The very next patient to try sirolimus after me was a five-year-old named Katie. She was diagnosed at only two years old, just when she was getting into princesses and beginning to experience the world, all those firsts, like digging in the dirt and playing with her older brother. But these experiences had to be avoided to protect her fragile and flighty immune system. Her doctor told the family that he hadn't had much experience with Castleman disease and had printed some shaky "information" off the Internet (the diagnostic criteria hadn't been published at this point). He knew enough, though, to understand that pedi-

atric cases of Castleman disease were even less well understood
and studied than adult cases. Katie's parents were understandably
terrified. Eventually, they reached out to the CDCN. We were
able to connect her with an expert in their area, but despite his
best attempts, nothing seemed to be working for Katie. Over
four years, she missed out on a lot of normal life. She endured
multiple unsuccessful treatments and fourteen hospitalizations.
She underwent a number of procedures, immunosuppressive
treatments, and chemotherapies. Still no reprieve. She began
receiving cytotoxic chemotherapy, which helped her symptoms
somewhat but limited her energy levels, restricted her growth,
and led to a serious side effect—hemorrhagic cystitis—which
landed her in the hospital and required nine weeks of continuous infusions through a PICC line to treat it. All of this occurred while her dad was back and forth for military deployments
to the Middle East.

After exhausting all other options, her doctor decided to try
sirolimus based on my case and data. Katie still isn't back to 100
percent and still has her bad days, but sirolimus has significantly
improved her quality of life over the last year and helped her to
avoid even a single hospitalization. She has more energy, she
runs, laughs, and plays more than she did in the previous four
years. The drastic improvement in her health meant that she had
the ability and the energy to graduate kindergarten. And Katie
even learned how to ride her bike this year. That's not a metric
we're going to track in a clinical trial, but it's as important as any
other for a parent. In short, she gets to be a kid again. Katie has
also inspired her mother, Mileva, to join the CDCN fight as the
volunteer leader of our patient engagement program; she does
everything from consoling family members of deceased patients
to motivating patients to join the fight.

Castleman disease was very personal to me early on in my
journey, because I was battling it. Now, Castleman disease is
even more personal to me, because I have developed so many

bonds with patients—like Katie—who have been affected by it. Seeing her doing so well brings me and my team so much joy.

So the next time sirolimus was used as a last-ditch effort, my hopes were even greater. Lisa, a fourteen-year-old girl in Colorado, went from perfect health, horseback riding, gymnastics, and track to utter misery in the ICU in a matter of days due to iMCD. All her organs were failing. She gained fluid everywhere. She lost consciousness. Blocking IL-6 didn't work. Carpet-bombing combination chemotherapy didn't work. A ventilator and dialysis machine were the only things keeping her alive. Her doctors decided to try sirolimus along with everything else. She showed the slightest signs of improvement before crashing again. Despite multiple rounds of chemotherapy and full-dosage sirolimus, Lisa couldn't survive her immune system's attack on her body. She passed away three months after she was admitted. Idiopathic multicentric Castleman disease won again. Nothing more could have been done, but that didn't make it any easier. Sirolimus may be my miracle for now, but it's clearly not everyone's. Among the first few iMCD patients treated with sirolimus that I'm aware of, some have improved and some have not. That's not good enough. The fact that it has worked for me (at least, as of my now typing this page) isn't enough.

Why does sirolimus work in some but not others?

What else is going wrong that could be targeted with a new treatment approach?

To answer these questions, I continue to work. I recently pulled together the T cell–VEGF–mTOR data into a grant application and was awarded funding by the NIH—the first-ever R01 or federal grant of any kind to study iMCD. We're applying the funds to push forward our understanding of T cells, VEGF, and mTOR in iMCD, including a clinical trial of sirolimus in patients who do not improve with siltuximab. We hope to understand the effectiveness of sirolimus in iMCD and uncover other potential novel treatment options.

A little while ago, I was reading through one of my medical reports when I noticed a code that I didn't recognize on the top of the page: D47.Z2. These International Classification of Disease, or ICD, codes come from the Centers for Medicare & Medicaid Services, and are part of the vast system for categorization that medicine relies on. I guess I could be forgiven for not recognizing D47.Z2, because there are some really obscure and precise codes—V91.07XD denotes burn injury by water skis on fire; V97.33XD indicates being sucked into a jet engine for a second time (a second time!); and W61.62XD means you've been struck by a duck, of all things.

Confused, I googled it: D47.Z2. It was Castleman disease. Our very own code.

When I was first diagnosed, no unique code existed for Castleman disease. It was always referred to with a miscellaneous code, one that covered a number of hard-to-categorize diseases. Not anymore. It's not that there was more demand (or supply) for repeat water-skiing-fire burns before I became ill. It's just that fewer people with Castleman disease were advocating for a code than individuals with water-skiing-fire burns. And it still wouldn't exist if Frits van Rhee, colleagues from the CDCN, and I hadn't lobbied the Centers for Medicare & Medicaid Services for it in 2014. Someone had to turn hope into action to make this a reality. If you don't do it, oftentimes no one else will.

We've come a long way.

Before the creation of the CDCN, the fight against Castleman disease was kind of like if American colonists were fighting one another when they were taking on the British (with apologies to my Oxford colleagues and British collaborators, "the British" represent Castleman disease in this metaphor). The colonists would have never fought off the British if they weren't unified. The CDCN pulls individual researchers together and recruits new researchers to pursue a unifying vision and game plan that achieves more than we could on our own.

Rather than performing studies that measure the levels of one molecule (e.g., IL-6) in the blood of a few Castleman disease patients, as had been done in the past, our collaborative network enables studies of biospecimens pooled from around the world that are measuring far more data points than ever before. Take the latest, for instance: Frits and I are currently analyzing results from a proteomics study that measured the levels of 1,300 proteins in 362 blood samples from 100 iMCD patients, 60 patients with related immunological disorders, and 40 healthy controls. Our initial review of the data suggests that our proposed model was correct in at least one way: iMCD involves many cytokines, and there's a lot more to it than IL-6. Remember: You can't see what you don't look for and you don't know what you don't measure. And the data also suggest that iMCD really does seem to sit at the intersection of autoimmunity and lymphoma. Frits and I now serve as cochairs of the CDCN's Scientific Advisory Board. He leads all efforts related to Castleman disease patient care and expert guidance; I lead our translational research efforts. We still frequently disagree on our interpretations of data, but that's so important in science. Our debates and discussions get us closer to the right answer. And sometimes we grab a beer together afterward. He's my colleague first, my friend second, and he also happens to be my doctor.

To ensure that the CDCN is poised to launch large-scale studies like the proteomics study, we've developed a multi-pronged strategy. We launched a biobank to continuously procure samples and patient data. These samples can be stored until the moment that our network crowdsources a brilliant new idea for a study or until enough samples are obtained for a study that was on hold. We still turn to our community of physicians and researchers to contribute samples, but we've learned it's much more efficient to go directly to patients for samples, just like we do for patient data in the registry study. Coordinating sample sharing between researchers' institutions requires immense effort and utilization of every negotiation, strategic decision making, and managerial economics course I took in business school. Fortunately, patients want to be a part of the solution and give of themselves, literally, through their blood and tissue samples. Patients often post on social media that the CDCN is their only hope for a cure and a normal life. But actually, it's those patients, who donate samples, data, and funds, that are the only hope the CDCN has for developing a cure.

We also partner with tech and pharmaceutical companies on large-scale studies whenever possible. One tech company, Medidata, is contributing machine learning and data science tools to help us generate clinically meaningful insights from the half a million data points in the proteomics study. Though they are often demonized because of a few notable bad actors, pharmaceutical companies have incredible power to do good through contributing funds, data, and samples for research. These are the essential building blocks for breakthroughs, and the effort needed to obtain these resources often limits the rate of progress. Moreover, they are the only players in biomedical research that can actually develop drugs to save patient lives. Saving lives is our end goal, and we don't ever forget it.

We've had several major breakthroughs for iMCD, and we have several high-impact studies in process with collaborators around the world to identify the cause, key cell types, communication lines, and possible new treatment approaches. The results of the CDCN's first multi-institution study, spearheaded with the viral hunter at Columbia University, indicate that a viral infection is not likely to be the cause of iMCD. Now, we've turned our attention to genetics and identified several mutations that are being investigated as possible causes of or contributors to iMCD. These leads were generated from another high-priority study on the CDCN's International Research Agenda: a genomic sequencing study, made possible by more than forty thousand dollars in donations from my Wharton classmates.

Multiple independent researchers are currently studying the potential role and effects of these genomic alterations in iMCD.

I'm one of those researchers studying genomic alterations in iMCD and also one of the patients in whom alterations in an immune regulatory gene have been identified. The gene of interest serves as an on-off switch for T cells. A mutation in this gene could explain my T cells spiraling out of control and my iMCD. But it's not very straightforward or easy to tease out whether this mutation is the cause or just a red herring; we all harbor thousands of rare variations in our genomes that have no consequences at all. Indeed, distinguishing the genetic variations that actually contribute to disease from the ones that don't is far more challenging than the proverbial needle in a haystack. This process is more like finding a single strand of hay that looks just like the other 3 billion strands of hay in the haystack—it would be great if it stood out like a needle!

We know that I inherited one copy of the mutated gene from each of my parents. We were able to determine my mother's DNA sequence ten years after her death because she had been in a clinical trial where a few tubes of her blood were collected but never studied. I knew about the trial and the tubes, because I held her hand while it was drawn (my mom, like my sister Lisa, didn't do well with needles). At the time, she had given her consent to allow for future research and sharing with outside researchers. I know she never imagined it would be her son who was doing the research or her baby boy who could benefit from the information contained in her blood samples, but I don't think either of us expected most of what has happened to our family over the last decade and a half.

One way to try to figure out when rare variations are predisposing us to or causing a particular disease is to introduce the exact genetic change found in the human with the disease into mouse embryos. Once the mice are born, we can compare their phenotypes or particular features with those of mice that are genetically identical except for the mutation. If the mice with the particular mutation demonstrate features similar to those of the humans with the disease, but the nonmutant mice don't, then you've nailed it. Ruth-Anne Langan, a PhD student in my lab, is currently studying mice with my exact mutations to investigate the gene's possible role in iMCD. We call these mice little Daves. We're hopeful that we're on to something but realistic that we still have a long way to go, especially since mutations in this gene have not been found in other iMCD patients as of yet.

I'm still contacted daily by physicians or patients asking what to do to treat Castleman disease and how the disease works. I say "we don't know" a lot less than before, but I'm still forced to say it. Perhaps one of the most gratifying aspects of my work is how we're sharing our network blueprints with other rare disease groups, so they can follow our steps toward building patient-centric, collaborative networks to crowdsource the most promising research. No more silos. We hope there will be less "we don't know" for other rare diseases too.

We also look to other diseases to leverage the good work that has already been done in studying them. Most directly, we review our research findings to propose candidate drugs already approved to treat other diseases as possible off-label treatments for Castleman disease. Consider that it took twenty-five years between the discovery of elevated IL-6 in iMCD and the first-ever FDA-approved treatment for iMCD targeting IL-6. Now, consider that approximately fifteen hundred drugs are already approved by the FDA for various diseases, which could be used tomorrow or even today for the first time ever to treat one of the approximately 30 million Americans with one of the approximately seven thousand rare diseases with no FDA-approved treatments. *How many lifesaving drugs already exist that are waiting to be applied to deadly diseases?*

Let me tell you about one.

When my uncle Michael was diagnosed with metastatic angiosarcoma, a rare cancer with a horrible prognosis, I accompanied him for a visit to a top sarcoma oncologist. My uncle was told that there were two treatment options and that he likely had about one year to live. I asked the doctor if he would send off my uncle's tumor for cancer genetic testing to search for a genetic mutation that could possibly be targeted with a treatment already FDA approved for other forms of cancer.

My uncle's doctor told me he wouldn't order the genetic test, because it rarely returned any useful information. Though it is informative to diagnosis and prognosis in a large proportion of cases, it impacts treatment selection in fewer than 10 percent of cases.

What if my uncle was in that fewer than 10 percent? I thought.

Then I asked if the doctor would perform a test of my uncle's cancer for something called PD-L1 and if the test was positive, consider treating my uncle with an FDA-approved inhibitor of PD-L1 or its receptor, PD-1. Programmed death–ligand 1 is often found on the surface of cancer cells as a result of cancer-causing genetic mutations and DNA damage. The cellular protein doesn't just hide the cancer from the immune system, it actually induces the death of immune cells that approach to try to kill the cancer cells. So inhibiting PD-L1 or its receptor in cancer patients in whom PD-L1 is increased allows the immune system to recognize and kill those cancer cells without being killed themselves. It would be a Hail Mary as to whether PD-L1 was elevated or if blocking it would be helpful for my uncle. The doctor explained that PD-L1 had not been studied in angiosarcoma or any other form of sarcoma and no drugs blocking PD-L1 or its receptor had been used in these cancers, so he wouldn't order the test or consider administering the drug.

"Even if it's positive, the drug probably wouldn't work and it's prohibitively expensive anyway," he went on.

But you don't know if you don't try, I thought. *Someone has to be the first. And you just told my uncle that he has limited time and options. How do you know what's prohibitively expensive to someone anyway?*

After the visit, I encouraged my uncle to find another oncologist who would order the tests, which he did. The sarcoma expert was right about one thing: The genetic test was unrevealing. There were no mutations in the genetic code of the cancer cells that could be effectively targeted with an existing treatment. However, my uncle's cancer cells were brilliantly positive for PD-L1. They were covered in it. Could blocking PD-L1 treat his cancer? Two drugs targeting the receptor for PD-L1 were already FDA-approved for lung cancer and melanoma. Soon thereafter, my uncle became the first angiosarcoma patient that we're aware of to take one of those drugs. He experienced a dramatic improvement in his symptoms, laboratory abnormalities, and tumor size. By the time this book is published, I hope that he'll be crossing three years in remission. Of course, he has no guarantees for the future, but "every day is a gift" according to my uncle Michael. This case has now led to off-label use and clinical trials of this drug and others like it in angiosarcoma, which we hope will help many more patients with this disease.

How many other drugs are there like this, just sitting on shelves in pharmacies? Unfortunately, few incentives exist for pharmaceutical companies to invest in expensive clinical trials to determine if an already FDA-approved drug may be effective for a rare condition. And when clinical trials are performed, the data are rarely submitted to the FDA for approval in this new use. The whole process is just too expensive and time-consuming. And there are potential downsides: If the drug elicits new side effects in the trial for the rare disease, its approval for the original disease is put at risk. We need to incentivize the study of already approved treatments for patients with no other options. Both my uncle and I are living proof that there could be many other options already out there for many patients, we just haven't discovered them . . . yet.

As I write this, I'm the healthiest I've been since I became ill, in 2010 (though I no longer exercise—not because I can't, but because I want all of my energy to go toward unmasking this disease and spending time with Caitlin and other loved ones). I had five deadly episodes in the first three and a half years after becoming ill. Since I took over my treatment, I haven't had a single relapse in five years, which is by far the longest stretch of health for me since my diagnosis. This remission is about seven times as long as my previous average remissions. I feel confident saying that sirolimus is extending my life. It is amazing to think that it had always been less than a mile away at my neighborhood pharmacy, but no one had thought to use it. Sometimes the answer is hiding in plain sight.

But the war is far from over. It's not the end, because we haven't cured Castleman disease yet and patients are still suffering from this disease. With recent media exposure, I get a lot of congratulatory emails for "curing your disease." Unfortunately, these are premature. No doubt, to use a football metaphor, we were backed up near our own goal line in 2012 and the game was basically over. But, against all odds, we have taken back the momentum and we're marching down the field. Today, we're approaching midfield. We're locked in on several promising leads. But the clock is ticking and we need help chasing our cure. We still have a ways to go—for me and for the thousands of other people in the fight of their lives with this disease. And I know that if we don't continue to push forward, no one else will.

And I know I'm not totally in the clear. My disease can come back at any moment. At the same time that I'm getting further from my last relapse, I'm likely getting closer to my next recurrence. But despite that, when I do get sick again, it won't be the same as before—because the medical community's understanding and treatment of iMCD have changed. And I've changed. I've learned the difference between being hopeful and being invincible in hope, as my mom's newspaper clipping said. There's a big difference, as big as the distance between wishing and doing. Knowing that I'm doing everything humanly possible to unlock the mysteries of this disease in the time before my next relapse helps me to worry less about when, and dare I say *if,* it will come. I won't have any regrets. I will have fought with everything I've got. And I will have enjoyed every moment of this journey chasing hope and life around the track.

I CONSIDER MYSELF to be very fortunate.

Not always in the literal sense—I've clearly had some pretty lousy luck in the health department. But my experience has liberated me to follow my passions and has given me peace, knowing that I'm making the most of every day while my clock is ticking. I have an incredible sense of purpose now, and I feel as though I have powers I never could have imagined before I got sick. Now I lead an army, and I get to watch people I've helped motivate strike back against the thing that almost killed me, and that continues to threaten and shorten lives around the world.

On August 19, 2018, my fortunes turned yet again. I rushed down the halls of Pennsylvania Hospital just as I had many times before—to perform CPR (unsuccessfully), to administer the umpteenth mental status exam to George and (successfully) reconnect him with his daughter, to get a power nap in Ben Franklin's old library. I even passed by the same security guard I had passed so many times in my early days working in the hospital. But this time was different. Caitlin and I were rushing down the halls together to deliver our first child, the newest AMF: Amelia Marie Fajgenbaum. Almost exactly eight years after I lay in the ICU wishing and hoping that I'd be able to survive so that one day I could have a family with Caitlin. And thirty-one years after Caitlin was born in the very same hospital. I got to see life, my daughter's life in the same place where I'd seen so much tragedy and where I'd sharpened my sword.

I have wept tears of joy only five times in my life: when my mom joked that she looked like the Chiquita Banana Lady after her brain surgery, when I learned of my mom's clean MRI scan during a freshman seminar at Georgetown, when Caitlin said yes to my proposal, when I finally began to turn the tide against Castleman disease with the addition of IVIg, and when I first laid eyes on Amelia. The joy hasn't stopped either—Amelia has brought more happiness to us in her young life than we could have ever imagined.

A lot had to occur for this to happen. Broadly speaking, I had to turn my hope for a future family with Caitlin into actions that enabled me to survive. I had to let Santa Claus go after I realized that what I needed wouldn't appear under the tree unless I put it there. More specifically, Caitlin had to accept me back into her life after I'd largely taken her for granted. And then she had to forgive my instructions to keep her from me when I first got sick.

By the time this book comes out, I hope it will be more than five years since I'll have last been sick. I can't be certain that will be the case. But I'm doing everything in my power to make sure that my hope turns into reality. I can't help but feel like this is a new overtime for me and my family.

ACKNOWLEDGMENTS

It may seem like my journey all came down to one decision that I made in early 2014. But it wasn't just one decision and it certainly wasn't just me. I literally wouldn't be here today if I didn't have a family who supported me and sustained me during my toughest moments. If I didn't first have a mother whose encouragement of my dreams and crazy ideas gave me the courage to question the status quo for my disease. If I didn't have an incredible army of CDCN physicians, researchers, volunteers, and supporters fighting alongside me. If so many other Castleman disease patients hadn't channeled their hope through us by giving their blood samples, medical data, and donations. If I didn't have so many people sharing words of encouragement and prayers as well as taking actions like visiting me when I was sick, attending CDCN events, and donating funding and time for research. These incredible people are helping to move their and my prayers closer to reality, making every second count, and creating silver linings along the way. I want to extend a huge thank-you to this great big group and say that your collective support has meant the world to me. If I've inadvertently left anyone out of these thanks, I am so sorry; I so appreciate everyone who has contributed to this fight.

First and foremost, I have to start by thanking my amazing wife, Caitlin; my father, Dr. David Fajgenbaum; sisters Gena Fajgenbaum Combs and Lisa Fajgenbaum; brothers-in-law Chris Combs and Michael Prazenica; and Bernie and Patty Prazenica—my in-laws—for your unconditional love during my toughest times, my happiest moments, and my journey chasing my cure. My beautiful daughter, Amelia, even before you were born, the dream of you inspired me to keep fighting. My dreams of being part of your future continue to inspire me. I am eternally grateful to my grandparents, Patrick and Grace Fitzwilliam and Harry and Claudia Fajgenbaum. You taught me that family is the most important thing in life. Grandad Paddy, your ascension from the mailroom to CEO was an example to me that anything is possible with hard work and respect for others. I am so thankful for all of my aunts, uncles, and cousins in Trinidad, who remind me of my mom and the importance of living a balanced life. My cousin Phillip Fajgenbaum, from the time you were a little guy helping out at Ravenscroft football games and wearing Georgetown gear, you've always been in my corner. Thank you. Uncle Michael Fajgenbaum and Aunt Sylvia Fajgenbaum, thank you so much for your hospital visits and support.

I consider myself so fortunate to have amazing friends who are like family. Your love has contributed in so many ways to my race for a cure. To my best friend, Ben Chesson, you've been a constant source of support, advice, and laughter ever since we were teenagers. It means so much to me that we're both godfathers for our firstborns. Kelli Chesson, thanks so much for always laughing at our jokes and being such a great friend to Caitlin and me. To my godmother, Charlotte Harris, and your family, Steve Harris, Stephanie Sneeden, and Conner Harris, the world is a better place with each of you in it, and I am grateful for your being examples to me of how to live a purposeful life. The Zuccato family, I'll never forget your believing in me and what the CDCN could achieve in our earliest days, even before I did. And you've contributed in so many ways to make our dreams become a reality.

Marjorie Raines, you are one of the most caring and generous individuals that I have ever met. Knowing your son David and the kind of person he is, I shouldn't have been surprised by how much you remind me of my mom. Your coming into my life when you did was one of my greatest blessings. Elana Amsterdam, you're the only person I know who enjoys talking about the immune system and cytokines as much as I do. And, even more, I love brainstorming with you about ways to translate study of the immune system into improved health for those suffering with immune system diseases. Tony Ressler, I won't soon forget meeting you for the first time at Georgetown. You saw potential in me as a leader and someone who could be inspirational to others, and I so appreciate your guidance and advice in helping to bring out some of the potential you saw. Glen de Vries, your relentless desire to help patients and to always ask what else you can do to support the Castleman disease fight—and then do it!—has meant more to me than I can ever put into words.

Although my time at Georgetown included my mom's death—the toughest experience of my young life—my Georgetown family helped me to work through my grief and have some of my best times. I'm forever indebted to Greg Davis, Liam Grubb, Ryan Dinsmore, Pete Fisher, Kate Fredrikson Windt, Matt Zambetti, John Lancaster, and Margaret Farland Griffin. Thank you for showing me how quickly strangers can become close friends and how that bond can last. Fran Buckley, as my "Georgetown mom" you have supported and looked out for me in ways that my mom would be thankful for. Dr. John

Glavin, you always pushed me to "think big," which inspired me to grow AMF beyond Georgetown. Dr. Bette Jacobs, you taught me everything I needed to know about compassionate leadership as the dean, a board member for AMF, and a board member for the CDCN. I am so grateful to Coach Bob Benson, Coach Joe Moorhead, Coach Rob Sgarlata, and all of my teammates on the 2003–2006 Georgetown football teams for the support you provided and life lessons you taught me. To all the members of the AMF family, which began at Georgetown and spread across the country, especially Marcie Gordon, Kiri Thompson, George Apelian, Allan From, Gary Hark, Tony Talerico, Pat Morrell, Josh Haymond, Tom Schaffer, Natasha Garcia, Ken Martin, Alison Malmon Mahowald, Phil Meilman, David Balk, Kelly Crace, Illene Cupit, Robin Lanzi, Heather Seruaty-Seib, Andrea Walker, Fran Solomon, and Kit McConnell, thank you for your support of me and grieving college students everywhere.

Like my time at Georgetown, my time at Penn Med was marked by the highest of highs and the lowest of lows. The "PMBC," led by Patrick Georgoff, Grant Garcia, Grant Mitchell, Ron Golan, Jeff Neal, Jason Hurd, Elisha Singer, Dan Kramer, Francisco Sanchez, Eamon McLaughlin, Ashwin Murthy, and Duncan Mackay, was always there to keep me smiling no matter what was going on. Penn Med faculty and leadership, such as Helene Weinberg and Drs. Jon Morris, Gail Morrison, and Arthur Rubenstein, helped me to get back on my feet after medical leaves so I could begin chasing my cure. Arthur, you took me under your wing and have guided me like a father.

At Wharton, Andrew Towne, Alex Burtoft, Alana Rush, Kathy Feeney, and June Kinney were the first five people I opened up to about my personal battle with Castleman disease. I was terrified to do so, but each of you not only made me feel supported but asked how you could help and then jumped into action. Andrew, I am so grateful for the countless hours you invested in brainstorming ways to overcome challenges, fostering the right culture within our CDCN team, and encouraging our classmates to get involved. Andrew, Alex, Alana, Kathy, and June, each of your examples helped to garner support from our entire class, which generated the early momentum the CDCN needed, and it undoubtedly changed the course of history for Castleman disease.

There are so many incredible people who built upon that momentum and pushed our work into uncharted territory. In addition to those already mentioned in the book, the efforts of the following have gone above and beyond: Helen Partridge, Michael Stief, Jenna Kapsar, Kevin Silk, Sophia Parente, Rozena Rasheed, Laura Bessen-Nichtberger, Kim and Nick Driscoll, Mary Guilfoyle, Craig Tendler, Jeff Faris, Emma and Andrew Haughton, Erin NaPier, Jasira Ziglar, Katherine Floess, Johnson Khor, Eric Haljasmaa, Mike Croglio, Amy Liu, Denise Leonardi, Martin Lukac, Ryan Hummel, Aaron Stonestrom, Colin Smith, Alex Suarez, Deanna Morra, Katie Stone, Cristina Kelly, Leo Adalbert, Julie Angelos, Michael Soileau, Molly Gannet, Steph Serafino, Sam Kass, Curran Reilly, Dale Kobrin, Wes Kaupinen, Greta Moretto, Alisa McDonald, Kate Innelli, Jenn Dikan, Nadine El Toukhy, Tony Forte, JC Diefenderfer, Ajay Raju, and Marc Brownstein. I also want to thank the full CDCN Board of Directors, Advisory Council, and Scientific Advisory Board, especially Drs. Frits van Rhee, Tom Uldrick, Corey Casper, Eric Oksenhendler, Amy Chadburn, Elaine Jaffe, Mary Jo Lechowicz, David Simpson, Nikhil Munshi, Gordan Srkalovic, Kazu Yoshizaki, and Alexander Fossa, as well as collaborators and mentors at Penn and beyond, such as Drs. Dan Rader, Lu Zhang, Vera Krymskaya, Kojo Elenitoba-Johnson, Megan Lim, Ivan Maillard, Angela Dispenzieri, Sunita Nasta, David Roth, Lynn Schuchter, Mike Parmacek, Larry Jameson, Dave Teachey, Dermot Kelleher, Mike Betts, and Taku Kambayashi. Taku, thank you for being such a great collaborator and co-mentor for Ruth-Anne. I want to thank Drs. Becky

Connor and Arnie Freedman for your dedication to sharing accurate and up-to-date information with Castleman disease physicians worldwide. I am thankful and honored for the opportunity to lead the Castleman Disease Center at Penn and the CDCN—to be a leader among such outstanding leaders—with each of you.

I also want to thank the rare disease leaders who pioneered the path forward and showed me that I could turn my hope into life-saving progress: Sharon Terry, Abbey Meyers, Josh Sommer, Emily Kramer-Golinkoff, Nicole Boice, Peter Saltonstall, and Drs. Phil Reilly, Leslie Gordon, Francis Collins, Stephen Groft, and Emil Kakkis. I also want to thank Tania Simoncelli, Samantha Scovanner, and Anne Claiborne for their commitment to rare disease patients and for being the most incredible partners in our joint mission to advance life-saving therapies for all rare disease patients. Chris and Gena, your relentless battle with ALS and unconditional love for one another inspires me every day and motivates me to continue to expand our work to other rare diseases in need of cures.

I am thankful for each of the doctors and nurses who cared for me and gave me hope for my future, including Clarice Dard, Norman Swope, and Drs. Frits van Rhee; Tom Uldrick, Adam Cohen, Alison Loren, Peter Voorhees, Preethi Thomas, Jeff Crane, Louis Diehl, and Jon Gockerman.

Reflecting on one's life and writing a memoir is both incredibly challenging and deeply rewarding. I am so thankful for the individuals who helped make this happen. William Callahan, thank you for always pushing me to unpack my emotions and for your guidance and keen insights in bringing my story to life. Richard Pine, thank you for your encouragement and visionary leadership of this entire process. You are one of a kind. Marnie Cochran, thank you for pouring your heart into this book and for making it so much fun along the way. Thank you for welcoming me into the Ballantine and Penguin Random House families with such open arms. Grant, Ben, Ryan, Lisa, Gena, and Caitlin, you all gave such great advice and feedback on drafts. It is because of these efforts that I have a legacy to pass on to my daughter should I not be here to tell her these stories myself.

Last, I want to thank you for reading this book! Each of us has challenges that we're facing. I hope you'll reflect on and find your "Castleman disease" or that thing that you're hoping for and passionate about, that motivates and inspires you. Something that will change the world, your world, or a loved one's world for the better. And if it happens to be championing Castleman disease, then that's great too (but not required)! We all have the tools, though some may need sharpening, to chase after and even solve these problems.

Turning hope into action isn't ever easy, and the fruits of such labor take time to develop. But you just have to start doing it. Start small. Do something. Anything you can to get closer to what you're hoping for, even if it seems like it's just routine paperwork. I hope you will never be mistaken for your father's pregnant wife, but if you are, try to use humor and positivity to get over that low point and the others we are all destined to face. And don't let the naysayer hobgoblins in the back of your mind stop you from getting started or from questioning the way things are done. My greatest regrets on my deathbed were actions I didn't take. Don't let those same regrets be yours. *Think it, do it.* And make every second count, because the truth is: We're all in overtime.

ABOUT THE AUTHOR

DAVID FAJGENBAUM (pronounced FAY-gen-bomb), MD, MBA, MSc, is one of the youngest individuals to be appointed to the faculty at the Perelman School of Medicine of the University of Pennsylvania. Cofounder and executive director of the Castleman Disease Collaborative Network (CDCN) and an NIH-funded physician-scientist, he has dedicated his life to discovering new treatments and cures for deadly disorders like Castleman disease, which he was diagnosed with during medical school. He is in the top 1 percent of youngest grant awardees of an R01, one of the most competitive and sought-after grants in all of biomedical research. Dr. Fajgenbaum has been recognized on the *Forbes* 30 Under 30 healthcare list, as a top healthcare leader by *Becker's Hospital Review,* and one of the youngest people ever elected a fellow of the College of Physicians of Philadelphia, the nation's oldest medical society. He was one of three recipients—including Vice President Joe Biden—of a 2016 Atlas Award from the World Affairs Council of Philadelphia. Winner of the RARE Champion of Hope science award, Dr. Fajgenbaum has been profiled in a cover story by *The New York Times* as well as by *Reader's Digest, Science,* and the *Today* show. Dr. Fajgenbaum earned a BS from Georgetown University magna cum laude with honors and distinction, an MSc from the University of Oxford, an MD from the University of Pennsylvania School of Medicine, and an MBA from the Wharton School. He is a former Division I college quarterback, state-champion weight lifter, and cofounder of a national grief support network.

Facebook.com/davidfajgenbaum or fb.me/davidfajgenbaum
Twitter: @DavidFajgenbaum

I hope that all Castleman disease patients and their loved ones will visit the Castleman Disease Collaborative Network website to learn more about the disease, opportunities to connect with other patients, and ways to contribute samples and data to the fight at www.CDCN.org

Anyone who is interested in donating to this life-saving research should also visit www.CDCN.org

You can email info@castlemannetwork.org for more information.

If you are a rare disease patient looking for guidance, please email rare@chasingmycure.com